IDIOT'S GUIDES.

AS EASY AS IT GETS!

Bike Repair & Maintenance

by Christopher Wiggins

ALPHA

A member of Penguin Group (USA) Inc.

ALPHA BOOKS

Published by Penguin Group (USA) Inc.

Penguin Group (USA) Inc., 375 Hudson Street, New York, New York 10014, USA • Penguin Group (Canada), 90 Eglinton Avenue East, Suite 700, Toronto, Ontario M4P 2Y3, Canada (a division of Pearson Penguin Canada Inc.) • Penguin Books Ltd., 80 Strand, London WC2R 0RL, England • Penguin Ireland, 25 St. Stephen's Green, Dublin 2, Ireland (a division of Penguin Books Ltd.) • Penguin Group (Australia), 250 Camberwell Road, Camberwell, Victoria 3124, Australia (a division of Pearson Australia Group Pty. Ltd.) • Penguin Books India Pvt. Ltd., 11 Community Centre, Panchsheel Park, New Delhi—110 017, India • Penguin Group (NZ), 67 Apollo Drive, Rosedale, North Shore, Auckland 1311, New Zealand (a division of Pearson New Zealand Ltd.) • Penguin Books (South Africa) (Pty.) Ltd., 24 Sturdee Avenue, Rosebank, Johannesburg 2196, South Africa • Penguin Books Ltd., Registered Offices: 80 Strand, London WC2R 0RL, England

International Standard Book Number: 978-1-61564-457-5
Library of Congress Catalog Card Number: 2013956273

16 15 14   8 7 6 5 4 3 2 1

Interpretation of the printing code: The rightmost number of the first series of numbers is the year of the book's printing; the rightmost number of the second series of numbers is the number of the book's printing. For example, a printing code of 14-1 shows that the first printing occurred in 2014.

Note: This publication contains the opinions and ideas of its author. It is intended to provide helpful and informative material on the subject matter covered. It is sold with the understanding that the author and publisher are not engaged in rendering professional services in the book. If the reader requires personal assistance or advice, a competent professional should be consulted. The author and publisher specifically disclaim any responsibility for any liability, loss, or risk, personal or otherwise, which is incurred as a consequence, directly or indirectly, of the use and application of any of the contents of this book.

Most Alpha books are available at special quantity discounts for bulk purchases for sales promotions, premiums, fund-raising, or educational use. Special books, or book excerpts, can also be created to fit specific needs. For details, write: Special Markets, Alpha Books, 375 Hudson Street, New York, NY 10014.

Trademarks: All terms mentioned in this book that are known to be or are suspected of being trademarks or service marks have been appropriately capitalized. Alpha Books and Penguin Group (USA) Inc. cannot attest to the accuracy of this information. Use of a term in this book should not be regarded as affecting the validity of any trademark or service mark.

Publisher: Mike Sanders

Executive Managing Editor: Billy Fields

Senior Acquisitions Editor: Brook Farling

Development Editorial Supervisor: Christy Wagner

Production Editor: Jana M. Stefanciosa

Senior Web/Graphic Designer: William Thomas

Indexer: Celia McCoy

Layout: Ayanna Lacey

Proofreader: Cate Schwenk

Photographer: Greg Perez

Contents

6   Chains
91

7   Hubs
109

8   Saddles and Seatposts
129

9   Pedals
149

10   Steering Systems
171

11 Frames 199

12 Suspension 217

13 Cranks and Bottom Brackets 223

14 Accessorizing Your Bike 247

15 Emergency Road Repairs 273

Appendix A   Glossary 278

Appendix B   Maintenance Schedules 282

Index 286

Introduction

If you think about some of your first glimpses of freedom, they likely came thanks to a bicycle. Mine allowed me to break the confines of my block. My editor's enabled her to pedal the cornfield-lined country roads around her home with her dog in tow. You probably had similar experiences.

Bikes make our world just a little larger and give us the freedom to saddle up and hit the road, whether that road leads around the neighborhood, to work and back, up and down trails, or somewhere yet to be determined. Wherever you're planning on riding, you need to know some essential maintenance and repair to keep your bike in good working order.

I've worked with some great bike mechanics over the years, and none of them went to bike repair school to learn what they knew. They all learned by doing, apprenticed to an older co-worker or bike shop owner. Years of practice and a passion for what they did honed the skills they have. You probably know someone like this. It's probably the person you turn to when you have problems with your bike. This book is in no way meant to replace those valuable assets.

Idiot's Guides: Bike Repair and Maintenance is meant to give you a greater understanding of the workings of your bicycle and to take some of the mystery out of how things work and why they do what they do. Armed with this knowledge, you should feel more in tune with your machine, better equipped to recognize problems, and confident in determining which repairs you can handle and when you might need some help. This understanding is something everyone who is passionate about cycling should have.

My hope is that the things you learn in the book will add years to the life of your bike, and the enjoyment you get from riding.

Now let's get our hands dirty.

Acknowledgments

I had a host of great people to learn from when I started in the bike business. I owe a debt of thanks to all those great mechanics. I learned something from every one of them.

I couldn't have done this without Kevin Duitsman. He is a great mechanic in his own right, and a better man.

To everyone in my family who has supported me through this career in the bike business, and the process of this book, this is as much for you as it is for me.

Chapter 1

Bike Basics

No matter the task, learning the basics first and then building on your knowledge is the best way to tackle something new. That definitely applies to bike repair and maintenance. In this chapter, you learn about some of the most popular types and styles of bikes, get a look at all the different parts that make up your bike, and gain an understanding of the tools you need to set up your home workshop so you can keep your bike in top shape.

Bike Types

It seems there are as many types of bikes as there are types of riders. All the choices can be confusing, but if you know the type of riding you want to do, you can better choose the best bike for you. Let's look at the most common types of bikes.

Road, or Racing, Bikes

Sometimes referred to as "10 speeds" (due to the number of speeds these bikes once had—they have more now), road bikes have narrow tires and drop-style handlebars. They're often used for racing, fast group, or training rides. They typically don't accommodate racks, fenders, or large bags. They're all about traveling light and fast! This is the type of bike featured most prominently in this book, with options shown for mountain bikes as well.

Mountain Bikes

Mountain bikes, which are most at home on dirt trails, have knobby tires and usually some form of suspension on the front and/or rear wheels. Traditionally, mountain bikes had 26-inch (66cm) wheels. Over the last decade, the "29er" has gained in popularity. Today, mountain bikes use the same-size wheel as the racing bike, 700c. The bigger wheel rolls faster and handles trail obstacles easier.

Comfort and Hybrid Bikes

At one time, if you didn't want the more aggressive position of a racing bike, you'd probably find yourself on a mountain bike. Customers would change the tires to something more suitable for pavement, and sometimes opt for a wider, more comfortable saddle, or seat. Manufacturers took note, and the comfort and hybrid bikes were born. These bikes have a much more upright riding position and are ideal for the casual rider. These bikes can be found with both 26-inch (66cm) and 700c wheels.

Fitness Hybrids

A relatively newer style of bike, the fitness hybrid shares characteristics with both hybrid and racing bikes. The handlebar position is between the two types, not as high as hybrid bikes and not as low as racing bikes, and the tire size is good for a variety of riding surfaces. You also have spots to mount fenders and racks. A fitness hybrid will take you through your first triathlon, to the store, to work, or down your favorite bike path. It's a great sporty, versatile bicycle.

Touring Bikes

During the bike boom of the 1970s, the touring bike was king. This bike has a longer wheel base and can fit wider tires and fenders. It's designed to carry loads both front and rear, with stability. While they never really went away, touring bikes have definitely been overshadowed by the flashier racing bikes. Touring bikes have been gaining popularity again over the last few years, however. As bicycle commuting has increased, riders have come back to a more versatile, durable machine.

Bike Anatomy

Before we get into actual repairs and maintenance, let's identify the various parts and pieces of your bike so you know what you're looking at (and so we're all using the same terms).

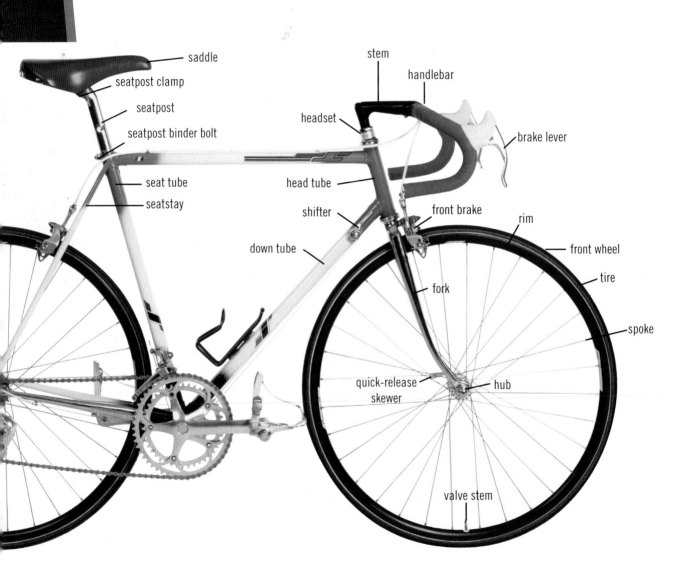

saddle

seatpost clamp

seatpost

seatpost binder bolt

seat tube

seatstay

stem

handlebar

headset

brake lever

head tube

shifter

front brake

rim

front wheel

tire

down tube

fork

spoke

quick-release skewer

hub

valve stem

rear tire

rear brake

top tube

bottom bracket

front derailleur

cassette

rear derailleur

chainstay

chain

crankset

chainring

pedal

Setting Up Your Home Workshop

Working on your own bike is one of the best things you can do. It gives you an appreciation and understanding of how your bike works and adds to the longevity of your machine.

You don't want to work on your bike in your living room, most likely. (Your spouse or roommates probably won't be keen on that idea either.) So you need a proper workshop, even if that's just a corner of your garage or basement. A dedicated work space is ideal, but not everyone has that kind of room. If you don't have a lot of room to spare, that's okay. You can make do with what you have.

Your space should be well lit. If the room doesn't have adequate lighting, try one or two clip-on spotlights. You can usually find them at auto parts stores.

You're going to be working with lubricants and solvents, and they sometimes don't smell all that great. So be sure you have adequate ventilation. It's better for you and everyone else in the area.

What's more, lubricants and solvents tend to drip. If you're working somewhere that might make a difference, use a mat or drop cloth under your bike to protect the flooring underneath.

You're also going to need some way to get your wheels up off the ground, at least the rear wheel. Good home repair stands cost a bit of money, but you might find they're worth it in the long run. A good work stand securely holds your bike, enables you to rotate the bike, and keeps you from having to work on the ground.

If you don't have the space for a full-size work stand, other options are available. A small, portable stand, for example, raises the rear wheel off the ground and is fine for most minor adjustments and cleaning. Best of all, you can stow it away when you're done or take it with you when you're traveling with your bike.

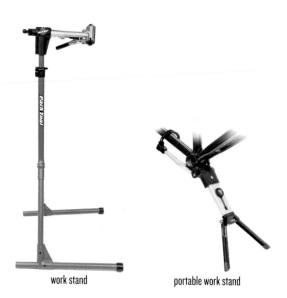

work stand

portable work stand

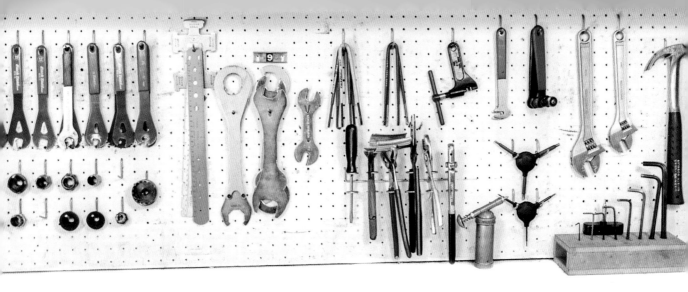

You're going to start amassing tools (if you haven't already), and you're going to need a place to put them. A standard-size tool box is handy for storing your tools and making them easily portable.

If you have more room, you might want to hang your tools on the wall. Pegboard works great for this. It's available at most home improvement stores, and you can find hooks in various sizes and lengths to hold your bike tools.

You don't necessarily need a workbench, but it's a really nice addition to a home shop. You can buy or even build a bench if you're handy. Your bench should be big enough so you can spread out your tools and parts. It also can serve as a place to store rags, rubber gloves, eye protection, and solvents.

If you're going to put in a workbench, consider adding a vise to it. A vise can help you securely hold tools and some bike parts. It also makes tasks like freewheel removal much easier.

At some point, you're probably going to get pretty grimy, especially as you work with lubes and solvents, so you should have access to water. A shop sink is nice, but a bucket and hose work just as well. After all, a clean bike is a happy bike.

Fishing tackle boxes are great for storing your bike tools and supplies. As a bonus, they're often less expensive than proper toolboxes.

vise

The Tools You Need

It might surprise you to learn that many of the tools bike shops use are the same ones you likely already have at home. Wrenches, pliers, sockets, screwdrivers—these are used in every bike shop, every day. Bike shops also use more specialized tools you maybe haven't seen or even heard of before. Let's look at some of the bike-specific tools necessary for your bike.

Tire Levers

Use these to pry the bead of the tire off the rim.

Freewheel Remover

This tool fits into the spline section of a freewheel, keeping it from spinning so you can remove it from the hub.

chain whip

cassette lock
ring tool

Cassette Lock Ring Tool and Chain Whip

Used in tandem, these tools enable you to remove a cassette from the freehub body of your wheel.

Cone Wrenches

Use these small, thin wrenches to adjust hub cones.

Pedal Wrench

This long, thin wrench provides enough leverage to enable you to remove and install pedals.

Although some of these tools are more specialized, you might already have Allen wrenches in your toolbox.

Allen Wrenches

Also called *hex keys,* these L-shape metric wrenches are useful on many parts of your bike. You also use them to install some accessories.

Bottom Bracket Tools

Bottom brackets come in several types, and specific tools are available to fit each one.

Headset Wrenches

If you have a threaded headset, you'll need these wrenches.

Crank Puller

You use this tool to remove crank arms from square, tapered, or spline-type bottom bracket spindles.

Chain Tool

Use this tool to remove your chain for cleaning. It also enables you to shorten new chains prior to installation.

Chapter 2
Wheels and Tires

Your bike's wheels and tires are often overlooked in importance. They quietly but efficiently respond to your input and give you a feel for the road or trail beneath you as you ride. In this chapter, you learn to identify the different parts of your wheels and tires, understand some important wheel safety issues, and discover some very basic tire maintenance procedures you can easily do yourself, including the repair you'll inevitably need at some point or another—fixing a flat.

Wheel and Tire Anatomy

Next to the frame, your bike's wheels and tires are the most important parts. What's the difference between the two? Wheels are the circular structures on which your tires, or the rubber pieces, fit. Wheels enable forward motion, and tires cushion the ride.

Your bike's wheel is made up of a *rim, spokes,* and *hub.* The rim is a hoop, usually made of aluminum, although some older bikes have steel rims and race wheels sometimes have carbon fiber rims. The hub is the center section of the wheel that connects your wheel to the frame. The hub houses the bearings that enable the wheel to spin and hold one end of the spokes; the other end of the spokes is threaded into a spoke nipple that sits in the rim. The rim has a hook on the inside that works with the tire bead to hold the tire in place, and the outside of the rim usually also has a sidewall that provides a surface for your brake pads.

Most bikes today are outfitted with a *clincher tire.* This type of tire is made of two *beads,* or hoops, made of steel or sometimes Kevlar. The body of the tire, or *casing,* is made of nylon cords. The tire is then covered in rubber, and the part of the tire that contacts the ground is the *tread,* which is thicker.

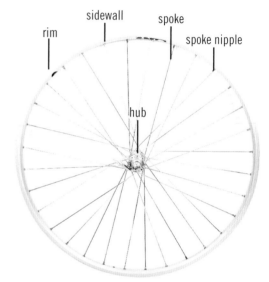

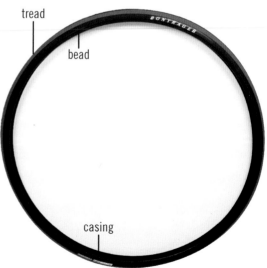

Axle Types

Your wheel is held onto your bike's frame by the axles. The axle is inserted into the wheel's hub, and the axle is bolted to your bike's frame fork. Axles should be straight and move smoothly within the hub.

hollow axles

solid axles

Axles can be solid or hollow. Solid axles use an axle nut to secure the wheel to the frame, and hollow axles utilize a quick-release skewer. Generally, quick-release axles are metric and solid axles are standard.

These systems are not interchangeable. A solid axle can sometimes be converted to a hollow, quick-release axle. But you should never try to thread a nut onto your quick-release axle.

hollow axles

solid axles

Most bikes made within the last 20 years use a ⅜-inch (9.5mm) axle. Some older bikes had front wheel axles that are ⁵⁄₁₆ inches (8mm).

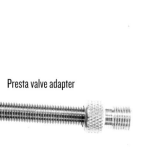
Valve Types and Rim Strips

Two types of valves are used on bicycles these days, the Schrader valve, which is the type of valve used on automobiles, and the Presta valve, or French valve.

Presta valve

Schrader valve

Presta valve adapter

The Schrader valve has an internal spring that keeps the valve closed. The Presta valve has an external nut you must open to allow air in the tube. Once the tube is inflated, the Presta valve nut must be closed to keep the valve from leaking air.

The Presta valve is generally seen as better for high-pressure tires. Their smaller size is more compatible with the narrower rims found on racing-style bikes, and because the Presta valve doesn't have an internal spring to close the valve, it can be easier to inflate with a mini pump.

If you have a bike with Presta valves but no compatible air source, you can use a Presta valve adapter. Loosen the nut on your valve, and screw the adapter onto the valve. You can then use any Schrader pump to inflate your Presta tube.

The purpose of the valve cap on Presta valve tubes is to keep the valve from puncturing the tube when it's folded inside your seat bag. After the tube is installed in a tire, the valve cap is unnecessary.

Now let's talk about rim strips. A rim strip covers the spoke nipples inside your rim and protects the tube from accidental puncture. Rim strips come in two types. A rubber rim strip is used with single-wall rims. A stronger rim strip, made of cloth or plastic, is used with double-wall rims.

On a single-wall rim, the nipple is on top of the rim bed. The rubber rim strip covers the nipples. A cloth rim strip won't stay in place on a single-wall rim. It will move and expose the spoke nipple, eventually causing a flat.

On a double-wall rim, the spoke nipple is inside the rim bed, between the two walls of the rim. A rubber rim strip isn't strong enough to withstand the pressure from the tube and will cause the rim strip and the tube to push into the spoke hole, causing a flat. The cloth strip is more durable and adds an extra layer of protection.

Using Quick-Release Skewers

Invented by Italian racing cyclist and inventor Tullio Campagnolo in 1927, the quick-release skewer enables you to remove your bike's wheels without the need for any tools. In order to be safe, however, it must be used properly.

acorn nut

cam lever

The quick-release skewer is made up of a cam lever on one side and a serrated acorn nut on the other.

With the lever open, you can tighten the acorn nut by hand until it takes a small amount of force—just enough to leave a momentary mark on your hand—to close the cam lever and secure the axle to the frame. When closed properly, the cam applies the force necessary to keep your wheel in the dropouts, or the slots in which the axle fits. You don't need to overtighten the skewer. A large amount of force when closing the cam lever just makes it harder to open the lever later.

Recently a new type of skewer has started showing up on bikes. This skewer, called a CLIX skewer, has a spring-loaded cup and a cam lever with a longer throw, or the amount the skewer opens when you open the lever. This enables you to remove the front wheel without loosening the acorn nut.

Usually, both skewers are on the left, nondrive, side. Due to interference from the front brake rotor, however, it's not uncommon for the front quick-release skewer on bikes with disc brakes to be located on the right side.

Especially on the front wheel, it's a good idea to have the lever pointing toward the rear of the bicycle. This prevents accidental opening if the lever gets caught on something.

The front forks on all modern bikes have tabs on the dropouts. These tabs were designed to hold the front wheel in the frame so it wouldn't fall off if the quick-release skewer was used improperly. With these tabs, removing and installing your front wheel takes a few extra steps. After opening the quick-release skewer, loosen the acorn nut by hand. When the nut is loosened enough to clear the tabs, remove the wheel.

When reinstalling your wheel, just reverse the process. Tighten the acorn nut until the pressure to close the cam lever is sufficient to leave a slight mark on your palm.

Removing Your Wheels

As you're just beginning repairing and maintaining your own bike, something like removing the wheels can seem like a daunting task. Many people are comfortable removing the front wheel but don't want to risk messing up the gears on the rear wheel. Removing the rear wheel is a simple procedure that seems more complicated than it really is.

Removing the Rear Wheel

1 With your bike in a bike stand, shift your rear derailleur so your chain is on the smallest cog. This makes removing and reinstalling your wheel much easier. If you don't have a bike stand, just lift the rear wheel off the ground by hand as you turn the pedals.

2 Open the brakes on your rear wheel. If you have caliper brakes, use the small lever on the side of the brake. For cantilever brakes, hold the brake arms against the rim with one hand and remove the ball end of the straddle cable from the brake arm with your other hand. For linear pull brakes, squeeze the brake arms with one hand while pulling out on the brake noodle with the other until it clears the noodle bracket. If your brake has a rubber boot, you might have to move it off the noodle to open the brake.

3 Open your rear quick-release skewer, or loosen the axle nuts on the rear wheel. Using your right hand, push the rear derailleur cage plate forward. This produces some slack in the chain you can work with.

4 With your left hand, remove the wheel from the frame.

To reinstall the rear wheel, just reverse the process. Push the cage plate forward and insert the rear wheel, placing the chain on the smallest rear cog. Pull the wheel up into the dropouts and then tighten the quick-release skewer. Close or reconnect the rear brake. Be sure the wheel is all the way into the dropouts and the wheel is centered.

Removing the Front Wheel

You remove the front wheel in much the same way as the rear, but it's easier because you don't have a chain or cogs to deal with.

You do, however, have to loosen the acorn nut on the quick-release skewer enough to clear the tabs on the dropouts.

Removing a Tire and Punctured Tube

Fixing a flat tire is the most basic bicycle repair. Flat tires generally happen in one of two ways. You can get a puncture when something penetrates your tire and tube from the outside, or you can get what's known as a pinch flat.

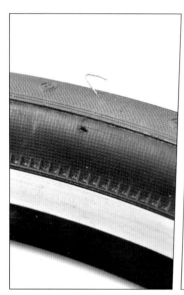 

1 Remove the wheel with the flat tire from your frame, and take a minute to visually inspect the tire. Punctures from small items like wire or staples will puncture your tube but usually don't require a new tire.

Large cuts or holes will require tire replacement. Be sure whatever punctured the tube isn't still lodged in your tire.

A pinch flat occurs when you ride your bike with insufficient pressure in your tires, and the tube gets caught between the tire and the rim. Two holes in the tube are a sure sign of a pinch flat.

2 To repair either type of flat, first insert your tire lever between the tire and the rim, and pry the tire off the rim.

3 If the tire is tight, use the hook end of a tire lever on one of your spokes. Then use a second tire lever to finish removing the tire from the rim. You only need to remove one side of the tire to remove the punctured tube from the tire.

Before you install a new tube, carefully run your fingers around the inside of the tire. It's possible something that wasn't visible from the outside penetrated the tire, and you need to clear that out so you don't install a new tube only to have another flat.

You're caught out on the road with a flat. You forgot your tire levers, and no one else is around. What do you do? In an emergency, you can use the lever from your quick release to pry the tire off the rim.

Patching a Tube

At some point, you might have to use a patch kit to fix a flat tire. Maybe you forgot your spare tube, or maybe your spare is flat. Having a patch kit—and knowing how to use it—can get you home, where you should replace your patched tube with a new one as soon as you can.

Patch kits are available in two types. One contains self-adhesive patches and the other contains glue. Each patch kit contains about six patches, a small piece of sandpaper, and a small tube of glue if the patches aren't self-adhesive.

Self-adhesive patches are a more convenient option because you don't have to worry about the glue drying in the tube before you've used all the patches.

glue patch kit

self-adhesive patch

For either type of patch, the tube must be clean and dry for the patch to adhere.

1 To patch a tube, first remove the tube, find the puncture, and use the sandpaper to lightly buff the area to be repaired.

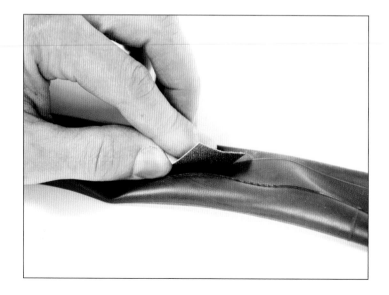

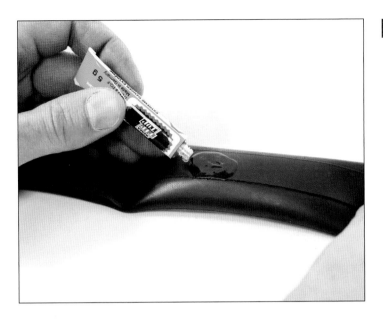

2 Spread a thin layer of glue around the hole, in an area slightly larger than the patch. Let the glue dry for a few minutes or until it's tacky to the touch.

3 When glue is dry, peel the backing off the patch and press the patch firmly onto the tube.

4 With the patch in place, reinstall your tube and tire.

If you're using a self-adhesive patch, simply buff the punctured area with sandpaper, remove the backing from the patch, and press the patch onto the tube.

Replacing a Tube and Reinstalling a Tire

Removing a punctured tube is the biggest part of the flat tire repair. Replacing a tube is easy, but it's not something to be done quickly. Take a little extra time so you don't get in a hurry and pinch the new tube. That only causes more problems.

1 To replace a tube, put just enough air in your spare tube to give it some shape. Doing this decreases your chances of pinching it as you reinstall it. If your tube has a Presta valve, you can do this with your mouth.

2 Insert the valve stem into the valve hole of your rim.

3 Work the tube into the tire so it's inside the tire, sitting smooth and not twisted or pinched within the tire well.

4 Starting at the valve stem, start working the tire back onto the rim by hand. The tire can get pretty tight when you get toward the end. Use the heel of your palm to roll the last part of the tire back onto the rim.

5 Push the valve stem up into the tire. This clears any of the tube that might have gotten caught in the tire during the installation. Pull the valve back down, use the Presta valve nut (if you're using Presta valves), and air up your tire.

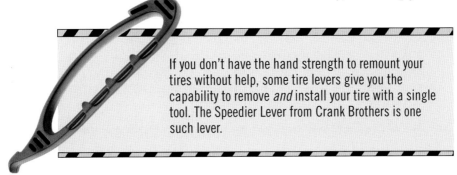

If you don't have the hand strength to remount your tires without help, some tire levers give you the capability to remove *and* install your tire with a single tool. The Speedier Lever from Crank Brothers is one such lever.

Working with a Spoke Wrench

When your wheels were built, the spokes were evenly tensioned within the rim manufacturer's guidelines, the rim was centered over the hub (this is known as "dish"), and the hub was centered in the rim. Failure to do any one of these things correctly and precisely would cause a "hop" in the wheel.

Wheel-building professionals use specialized tools like a truing stand, a dishing tool, and a spoke tension meter to get everything just right. For the adjustments you'll likely need to make, though, a spoke wrench is sufficient.

Working with a spoke wrench is part mechanics and part art. Putting too much tension, or uneven tension, on your spokes can do irreparable damage to your wheel.

Spoke wrenches are sized specifically for different sizes of spoke nipples. Some wheel manufacturers use a proprietary nipple; if you have one of these wheels, you need a special spoke wrench.

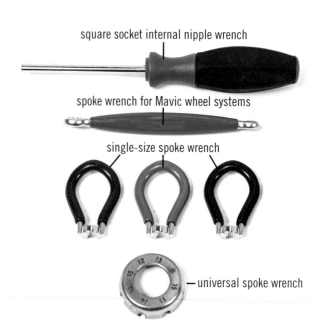

square socket internal nipple wrench

spoke wrench for Mavic wheel systems

single-size spoke wrench

universal spoke wrench

The number of spokes in your wheel has an effect on spoke tension. The fewer the spokes in the wheel, the higher the starting tension and the bigger the change will be.

If your wheel has bladed spokes, you need an additional tool before you start. This slotted tool holds the spoke in place so it doesn't twist as you loosen or tighten the spokes.

When adjusting spokes, use the brake pad as a guide, and watch to see which way the bend is causing your bike's rim to move. If it's off to the drive side, you need to tighten the spokes on the nondrive side at the affected spot. Tightening the spokes opposite of the bend pulls the rim back toward center.

Affix the spoke wrench to a spoke at the nipple. To adjust, start with a quarter turn at a time—remember, spoke nipples are right-hand thread—and pay attention to what the wheel does after you adjust the spoke. When the wheel is straight, you're done. If the bend moves over to the other side of the wheel, you went too far.

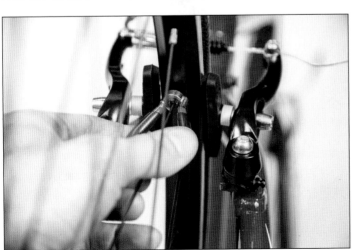

I recommend starting with an old wheel to get an idea for how the spoke tension feels and how the spoke wrench works. Getting that practice enables you to hone your skill without doing damage to your good wheels.

The Importance of Proper Inflation

Inflation and tire pressure are two of the most misunderstood aspects of riding a bike. Tire pressure has a big effect on not only comfort and enjoyment, but also tire and wheel longevity.

A common misconception is that a tire at max pressure has lower rolling resistance. On a perfectly smooth road this might be true to a point. But few of us ride on perfectly smooth roads, and an overinflated tire on real-world roads actually increases rolling resistance due to increased vibration. Your tire needs to be able to conform to the bumps and cracks in the road. An overinflated tire is also more likely to pick up debris and be cut by sharp stones.

But you also don't want too little pressure. A tire that's not inflated enough won't support your weight. This will lead to pinch flats or damage to your rim.

Every tire has a range of pressures printed on the sidewall. These are the recommended inflation pressures for that specific tire.

When pumping up your tires, start with a pressure that's somewhere in the middle of the range given. Then factor in your weight. Riding the same tire, a 110-pound (50kg) woman should not use the same pressure in the same tires as a 200-pound (91kg) man. In general, a lighter-weight person needs less air pressure than a heavier person riding the same bike.

Also keep in mind that not all tires are created equal. The construction of a tire affects the way it rides and to what pressure you should inflate it.

A tire with a reinforced sidewall and tread resists punctures and lasts for many miles. The ride might be quite stiff, but you can run this type of tire at a slightly lower pressure to improve the ride. The extra material in the tire maintains the tire integrity. If you spend most of your time commuting, riding on a variety of terrain (roads, crushed-stone bike paths, gravel, etc.) or roads with a lot of debris, this is the type of tire for you.

A very supple tire gives a very good ride, but it might not be as durable or long-lasting. These tires need to be run at a higher pressure to maintain tire integrity. If the weight of your tire is a concern, if you ride only "clean" roads, or if you race, this is a good option.

Chapter 3

Brakes

You probably don't spend a lot of time thinking about your bike's brakes ... until they stop working properly. Yet for obvious reasons, you need to give them some thought every now and then and be sure they're always in good working condition so they'll be there for you when you need them. In this chapter, you get to know specific types of brakes found on today's bikes and learn how to install cables, adjust the most common types of brakes, and perform some basic but key preventive maintenance.

Types of Brakes

Modern brakes are light, efficient, and powerful. In fact, they work so well, so often, you might not give them much thought. But as relatively problem free as today's brakes are, they do require maintenance. Cables stretch, pads wear, and pivots need to be kept clean and moving freely.

The most common types of bicycle brakes are caliper brakes, cantilever brakes, linear pull brakes, and disc brakes.

Caliper Brakes

Caliper brakes (also called side pulls) are mounted with a single bolt above the wheel, and arms extend down and around the tire and squeeze shut when the brake is applied. Older bikes could have a single-pivot brake, but dual-pivot brakes are now the norm.

On a single-pivot brake, each arm operates independently by a spring. Because of this, centering this type of brake can sometimes be a challenge.

A dual-pivot brake has a rotating piece called a cam that connects the two brake arms, allowing equal amounts of travel when applied. This type of brake is most often found on road bikes.

Cantilever Brakes

Cantilever brakes utilize one main cable that attaches to a straddle, or yoke. Two independently operating brake arms connect by a straddle cable. These brakes are attached to the bike by brake studs, or bosses, on the fork legs, or frame.

Cantilever brakes were found on most mountain bikes up to the mid-1990s and are still found on some touring bikes and cyclo-cross bikes.

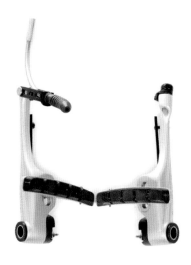

Linear Pull Brakes

An improvement over the standard cantilever brake is the linear pull brake (or Shimano V Brake). This brake attaches with a single cable, doing away with the straddle cable. The arms of the linear pull brake are longer, which allows the cable to clear the tire and provides for more powerful braking. Linear pull brakes use the same bosses as cantilever brakes, but because they pull more cable than a standard cantilever brake, they require a different brake lever.

Linear pull brakes are now the standard brakes found on hybrid, comfort, and entry-level mountain bikes.

Disc Brakes

Disc brakes provide much more efficient braking in wet or muddy conditions. With a disc brake, the rotor is mounted to the wheel's hub and the brake caliper is mounted to the bike's fork or frame. These brakes are available in both cable actuated and hydraulic.

Disc brakes were once mainly found on bikes like tandems, where heat buildup on rims was a concern, and on high-end mountain bikes. Now disc brakes can be found on mid-priced mountain bikes, cyclo-cross bikes, and soon on racing-style road bikes as well.

Setting Up Caliper Brakes

The caliper brake is the standard brake used on all racing-style bikes. The combination of a single cable and simple pad setup makes these the easiest of all brakes to set up and adjust.

1 Insert the cable into the brake lever, through the housing, and to the brake.

> Before you attempt to adjust any brake, be certain the wheel is aligned and centered in the frame. Adjusting a break to an off-center wheel means you'll have to readjust the brake later, after you adjust the wheel.

2 Insert the cable through the cable stop and anchor bolt. For the time being, leave the cable loose. Most bikes have a notch in the middle of the anchor bolt assembly; route the cable through this notch.

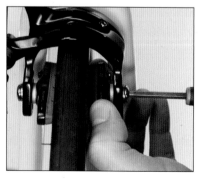

3 Center the brake. You can adjust dual-pivot brakes by hand, but older single-pivot brakes might be more difficult. If the brake center bolt has flats, slightly loosen the center bolt and use a small Allen wrench to move the brake caliper. Holding the brake caliper in place, retighten the brake center bolt. If the brake center bolt has no flats, loosen the center bolt, readjust the brake by hand, and retighten the brake center bolt.

4 Squeeze the brake caliper together by hand, give the cable a gentle pull to be sure it's positioned properly, and snug the cable. You don't want the brake pads to move as you tighten them in place, so squeeze the brake lever to hold the pad. Loosen the brake pad and adjust so the top of the pad is 1 or 2 millimeters from the top of the rim and as much of the pad touches the rim as possible. Tighten the pad and release the brake lever. Hold the brake pad with one hand and give the bolt a final turn to ensure it's tight. Repeat the process with the pad on the other side of the brake.

5 Both pads should move an equal distance. If you squeeze the brake lever and see your rim move, the brake isn't centered. On a dual-pivot brake, you can make fine centering adjustments by loosening or tightening the small screw at the top of the brake. The entire brake pad should be in contact with the rim. Otherwise, you'll get uneven pad wear and decreased braking performance.

6 Cut the cable and crimp the end to prevent fraying.

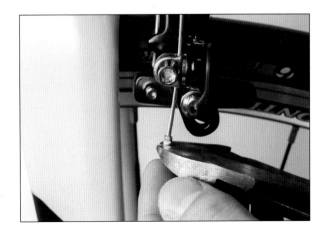

Setting Up Cantilever Brakes

Cantilever brakes are a solid option when you need a powerful brake with clearance for wider tires. These brakes use two cables, whereas many other brakes use only one. Cantilevers also feature two independently operating arms connected by a secondary straddle cable. The capability to use a standard road bike brake lever has made these brakes a natural choice for touring and cyclo-cross bikes. Let's look at the set up and adjustment for this type of brake.

1 Insert the cable into the brake lever.

2 Run the cable through the cable housing, through the cable stop, and to the brake.

3 Install the cable straddle (or yoke) onto the cable. This requires two wrenches, generally an open, or box, metric wrench for the back of the bolt and a hex key for the front. Position the straddle so it's in line with the center hole of the brake bridge, or hole in the fork crown (if your bike has them). Set the straddle so the straddle cable is at a 45-degree angle.

4 When placing the straddle, be sure to account for any accessories you have on your bike. The straddle shouldn't interfere with any fender or rack mounts, for example.

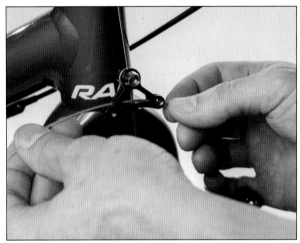

5 Run the cable through the straddle.

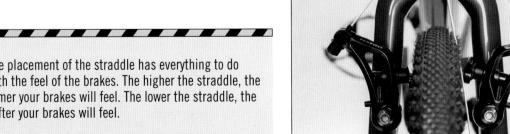

The placement of the straddle has everything to do with the feel of the brakes. The higher the straddle, the firmer your brakes will feel. The lower the straddle, the softer your brakes will feel.

6 Tighten the straddle bolt.

7 Attach the cable to the brake arms, inserting it through the washers and into the notches in the anchor bolt, and tighten the bolts to secure.

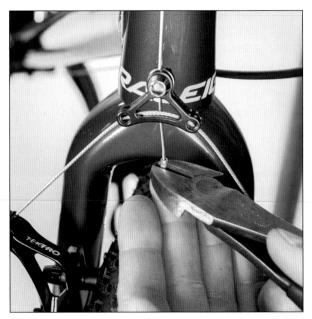

8 Cut the cables and crimp the ends to prevent fraying.

9 Loosen the brake pad bolts and set the posts so the pads sit slightly below the braking surface, if possible. Ideally, you want as much pad in contact with the rim as possible, so adjust the pad angle so the pads hit flush. This decreases the likelihood of the pads slipping under the rim if they come out of adjustment or get excessively worn.

10 If your brakes aren't centered, check to ensure your wheel is straight and aligned. If your brakes still need to be centered, use the spring adjustment screws on the side of either arm to make fine adjustments. Most cantilever brake bosses have three small holes that hold the brake spring. The spring tension of the brake is determined by which position is used. The top hole provides the highest tension; the bottom hole, the lowest. Most brakes perform best in the middle position. Both brakes should use the same position.

adjust the spring adjustment screw

Each brake arm should move smoothly on their bosses. If you've got a brake that's not moving freely, remove it from the brake boss. Be sure the boss is clean and well greased, and reinstall the brake.

Some brakes make some noise when the pad hits flush. To avoid this, you can "toe in" the pad, or make it so the front of the pad hits before the rear. Loosen the brake pad bolt and slide an emery board or something equally slim between the back of the pad and rim. Squeeze the brake lever to keep the pad in place, and tighten the pad. You're looking for only 1mm difference between the front and back of the brake pad.

Setting Up Linear Pull Brakes

Linear pull brakes (or Shimano V Brakes) have a simpler design that does away with the straddle and straddle cable. Instead, linear pull brakes use a single cable that attaches to one brake arm. Installed on the cable is an aluminum "noodle" that connects to a carrier on the opposite brake arm. The easier setup and better braking have made these brakes very popular on hybrid and comfort bikes.

These brakes pull about twice as much cable as a traditional cantilever or caliper brake. Because of this, a special brake lever must be used. Don't try to use a standard road brake or cantilever brake lever with a linear pull brake.

1 Rotate the barrel adjuster at the brake lever to line up the slots. Insert the cable end into the lever.

2 Run the cable through the housing and to the brake.

3 With the cable installed, rotate the adjuster to keep the cable from slipping out.

4 Slide the cable into the noodle.

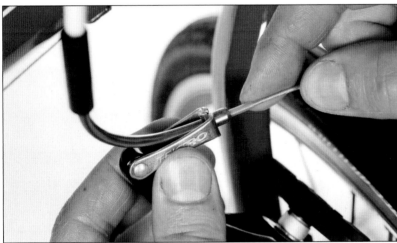

5 Insert the noodle into the carrier.

6 If your brake came with a rubber boot, position it between the brake arms.

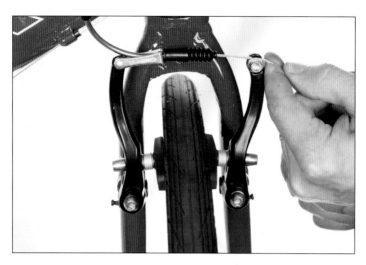

7 Insert the cable through the anchor bolt assembly, and pull the cable tight enough to get the pads close to the wheel's rim.

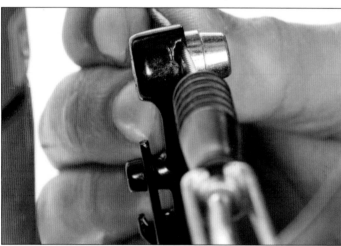

8 Be sure to get the cable in the anchor bolt groove.

9 Snug the cable with the anchor bolt.

10 Loosen the brake pad bolt and set the post so the pad sits slightly below the braking surface, if possible. Ideally, you want as much pad in contact with the rim as possible, so adjust the pad angle so the pad hits flush.

11 Cut the cable and crimp the end to prevent fraying.

12 If your brakes aren't centered, check to ensure your wheel is straight and aligned. If your brakes still need to be centered, use the spring adjustment screws on the side of either arm to make fine adjustments.

Some brakes make some noise when the pad hits flush. To avoid this, toe in the pad so the front of the pad hits before the rear. Loosen the brake pad bolt, and slide an emery board between the back of the pad and rim. Squeeze the brake lever to keep the pad in place, and tighten the pad. You need only 1mm difference between the front and back of the brake pad.

Setting Up Disc Brakes

Hub-mounted disc brake rotors are becoming a common sight on bicycles. The wet-weather stopping power that made them ideal for mountain biking also makes them a good choice for other types of riding. Once only available in hydraulic form, cable-operated disc brakes are now the norm. Here you learn how to set up and adjust cable-actuated disc brakes.

1 Insert cable end into the carrier in the brake lever.

2 Line up the slot in the barrel adjuster and insert the cable into the lever, though the housing, and back to the brake.

3 Turn the barrel adjuster so the cable can't fall out.

4 Run the cable through the housing and into the brake caliper cable stop.

5 Be sure the cable sits in the groove on the brake caliper.

If you're having trouble centering the brake, check to be sure your rotor isn't bent.

6 Insert the cable through the anchor bolt, put some tension on the cable, and tighten the anchor bolt.

7 At this point, the caliper should be centered over the rotor. If it isn't, loosen the caliper mounting bolts and move it into place by hand. When the caliper is centered, tighten the caliper mounting bolts.

8 With a cable-actuated disc, only one pad moves when you squeeze the brake lever. Using the stationary pad set screw, move the pad until it's close to the rotor but not rubbing.

Check the brake by squeezing the brake lever. You want the lever to move enough for good leverage without bottoming out. If the lever moves too much, move the other brake pad closer to the rotor. Make big adjustments by tightening the cable, and make fine adjustments using the brake adjustment barrel. When the adjustment is where you want, cut the cable and crimp the end to prevent fraying.

Most hydraulic disc brakes do not have an adjustment barrel for adjusting pads. However, you can adjust the calipers of these brakes in the same way you would a cable-actuated brake.

Manufacturers recommend replacing brake pads when only 1mm of the pad remains. Never touch the braking surface of the pad or the rotor with your bare hands. Oils from your skin can contaminate the pads and negatively affect braking performance.

Cable Lube and Maintenance

Neglected cables can cause problems with brakes. When you pull your brake lever, the cable should more freely and easily. Checking and lubing your cables from time to time lengthens their lifespan and keeps everything running smoothly.

If your brake cables run outside the frame, cable maintenance is quick, easy, and often doesn't require any tools.

1 Open or disconnect the brake. If your brake has a rubber boot, move it off the noodle to open the brake.

2 While squeezing the brake arms, pull the noodle to remove it from the carrier.

3 With the slack now in the cable, you should be able to slide the housing from the brake lever and expose the cable.

A missing cable crimp end will eventually lead to a frayed cable. If you catch it early enough, it's a simple task to cut the frayed end and crimp on a new cable end. If you don't, you'll have to replace the cable.

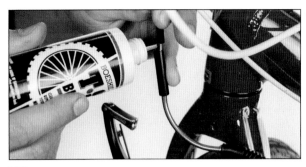

4 Apply a small amount of lube to the exposed cable—almost any drip chain lube work. Because it doesn't attract as much dirt, opt for a dry lube.

5 The noodle used on a linear pull brake can be a big sticking point because of its tight bend. If you're using these brakes, put a few drops of lube in either end of the noodle.

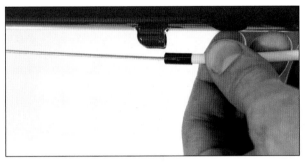

6 As you repeat the process with the rear brake, remove the housing from the cable stop on the top tube.

7 Lube the rear cable, paying special attention again to the noodle.

8 Back up at the brake lever, slide the housing to one side, and inspect the cable.

9 Apply a small amount of lube to the exposed cable. When you've finished, reattach your brakes and wipe off any excess lube.

Troubleshooting

When brakes stop working, it can be tough to know where to start to diagnose the problem. If they were working the last time you rode the bike, it's probably something pretty simple. So let's start at the front of the bike and work our way back.

Deviated Wheel

First, be sure your wheel is straight. Put your bike on the ground, and open the quick-release skewer. If the wheel wasn't straight, you'll feel it move. Close your skewer and check your brakes again. Oftentimes, that's the easiest fix to a brake problem.

wrapped cable

Twisted Handlebars

Sometimes handlebars can get spun around, especially if you pick the bike up by the handlebars after it's fallen over. When this happens, the brake cable can become twisted around the stem, causing the brakes to lock up. The solution is simple: just spin the handlebars around the opposite way, and the brakes should work again.

Cable Out of Lever

You disconnected your brake, removed your wheel, and when you put everything back together, you couldn't reconnect the brake. More than likely, the housing slipped out of the barrel adjuster on the brake lever. Just slip the housing back into the barrel adjuster, and everything should be fine.

Housing Out of Cable Stop

A similar situation can occur when the brake
cable housing slips out of one of the cable stops
on the frame. In this situation, there's not
enough tension on the cable, and your brake feels
mushy. To fix, disconnect the brake and put the
housing back in place.

Stuck Noodle

When reconnecting a V brake, sometimes the
noodle gets stuck and doesn't insert fully into the
carrier. This can cause both pads to drag. To fix,
adjust the noodle back into place.

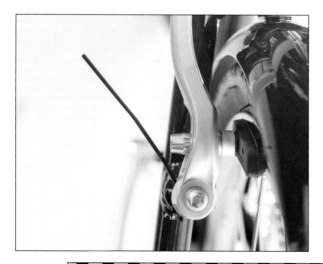

Sprung Spring

If just one arm of your brake is dragging, check
to see that the spring hasn't slipped out from
behind the brake arm. If it has, push the spring
back into place behind the brake arm. (It might
be easier to do this with the brake disconnected.)

Wipe your rims off every now and then with a clean rag. Dirt on rims and brake pads leads to
accelerated wear on both. Never use any kind of lubricants on your bike's braking surfaces.

Chapter 4

Shifters and Derailleurs

Think about how many times you use your shift levers during the course of a ride. This area of your bike gets a lot of use—and, therefore, a lot of wear—and requires a little more of your attention. In this chapter, you get a closer look at the workings of your shifters and derailleurs. You learn about adjusting your shifting system, as well as how to replace and maintain your shift cables for optimum performance.

How Shifters and Derailleurs Work

The way bikes shift today is really pretty amazing. You move the shift lever, it clicks, and then a quick and precise shift takes place. The derailleur gets most of the credit, but the underappreciated shifter does the majority of work.

The derailleur, although mysterious, really only has one function: it moves the chain from side to side. The rear derailleur has one additional function in that it employs two pulleys to keep tension on the chain as you shift to a smaller cog.

On both front and rear derailleurs, the chain runs through a cage. As the derailleur moves, the chain is "derailed" and either drops down on a smaller chainring or is pushed until it runs up onto a bigger chainring. Due to the relatively small difference in size from one cog to the next, shifts at the rear derailleur happen quite quickly. Because of the larger size difference of the front chainrings, ramps and pins aid in shifting the chain. The chain is pushed against the bigger chainring, and the ramps and pins lift the chain and finish the job.

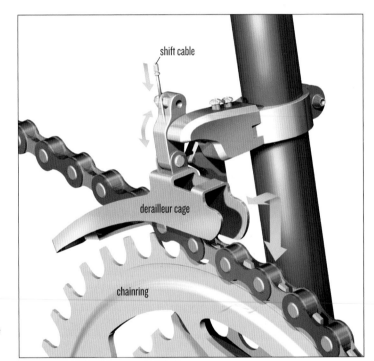

shift cable

derailleur cage

chainring

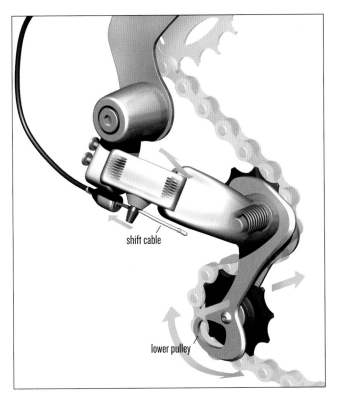

shift cable

lower pulley

How does the derailleur know how far to move with each click? Especially with the rear derailleur, the shifter makes the gear changes happen. Indexed, or "click," shifting is achieved when the shifter is built with stops that allow the shifter to move only a set distance for each click, enabling it to pull a specific amount of cable to shift the chain to the next gear.

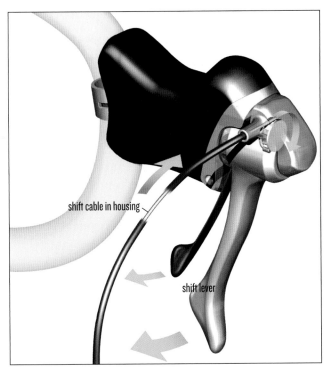

shift cable in housing

shift lever

A correct shift depends on cable tension. The shifter always moves the cable the same amount, but if the derailleur cable is too loose or too tight, the derailleur alignment is off and, therefore, the shift is off, too.

Before index shifting, we used "friction" shift levers. There were no detents, and you decided how far to move the lever. Because of this, you could mix and match shifters and derailleurs. Now manufacturers design components to work together and operate as almost a "closed system," using either proprietary cassette spacing, cable pull, or both.

Types of Shifters

Today's shifters are very much like the command center for your bike. Combined, or in close proximity with your brake levers, all the command and control you need is right at your fingertips.

Down-Tube Shifters

For decades, the shifters on road bikes were found on the down tube. While these shifters were light and simple, you had to take your hands off the bars to shift. Current shifters—such as dual-control, bar-end, twist, and trigger shifters—have made shifting more accessible and convenient.

Dual-Control Shifters

The shifter you're most likely to find on bikes today is broadly known as a *dual-control shifter*. This shifter marries the brake lever and shifter in one package. It enables you to shift and brake with the same lever without ever taking your hand off the handlebar. If the bike has a drop-style road handlebar, it likely has this type of shifter.

Bar-End Shifters

Some touring and cyclo-cross bikes still use a bar-end shifter. As the name implies, these shifters are installed in the end of a drop handlebar. They're still used because of their simplicity and reliability. They also have an option for friction shifting should you encounter a problem on the road you can't fix.

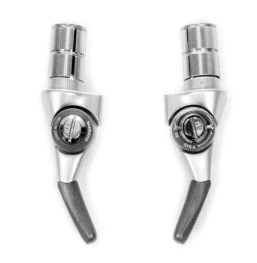

Twist Shifters

The twist shifter, or Grip Shift, was developed in the 1980s and provided an alternative to thumb shifters. They're light, have few moving parts, and are still in use on bikes and sold at a range of prices.

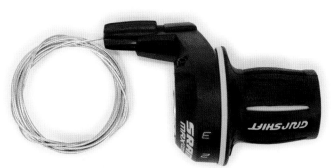

Trigger Shifters

The trigger shifter is commonly seen as an improvement over twist shifters. These shifters feature two paddles you operate with either your thumb or your thumb and index finger. Like the twist shifter, they're available in a wide range of prices.

STI Lever Maintenance

The Shimano STI (Shimano Total Integration) lever has been widely used on road bikes in all price ranges for the last 20 years. As widely accepted as these levers are, they're not problem free.

Older versions of the Shimano STI lever and some trigger shifters can malfunction after periods of inactivity. The grease used during assembly can become hard, prohibiting the lever's ratcheting mechanism from engaging. If your bike doesn't shift, and you don't hear or feel a "click" when pressing the shift lever, this may be the problem.

Flushing the shifter with a solvent like White Lightning Clean Streak can sometimes repair the shifter. Pick a spot that's well ventilated and where dripping solvent won't ruin the floor.

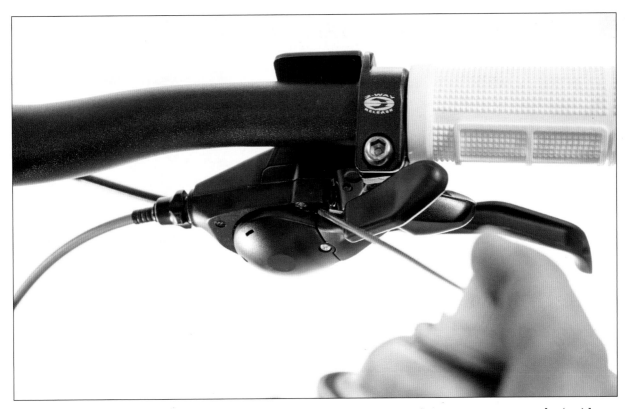

If you have a road bike, squeeze the brake lever, and look for a spot where you can access the inside of the lever. (Don't try to disassemble the shifter.) Spray a good amount of solvent into the lever, and work the lever back and forth. It might take a couple applications until it starts to work again.

Some trigger shifters have a top plate you can remove to make applying the solvent easier. If your shifter doesn't, find a spot near the lever itself to apply the solvent. Again, it sometimes takes a good amount of solvent to flush out the shifter. The longer the period of inactivity, the harder it might be.

You might need to let the solvent sit overnight before you see a change.

If these methods don't work, there is another, albeit extreme, option. You can remove the lever from the bike and soak the shifter in mineral spirits. A full 24-hour soak should be enough to dissolve the material causing the shifter to malfunction. For a road lever, you *must* remove the brake lever hood before you do this.

Cable Housing Differences

On modern bikes, every cable runs through at least one piece of cable housing—basically a plastic-coated steel tube that carries and protects the cable. The exterior plastic protects your bike and also protects the cable from moisture. There's usually also a plastic sheath inside the housing to help reduce friction on the cable.

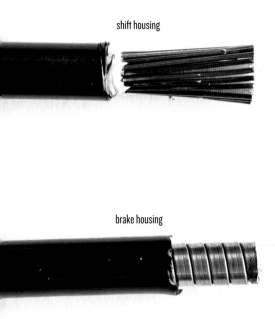

shift housing

brake housing

Your bike likely has two types of cable housing—brake housing and shift housing.

Brake housing is made up of a coil of steel that provides the compression the cable needs for braking. The cable pulls, and the housing pushes; both parts are equally important. As brake housing bends, it changes length slightly and can pull the cable. Notice what happens to your rear brake, for example, when you turn your handlebars as far as they'll go. This isn't a problem because you wouldn't make this kind of turn when riding, but this change in length is unsuitable for indexed shifting systems.

In compressionless shift housing, steel wires run parallel inside the housing. The housing does not change length when flexed and provides consistent shifting.

A cable cutter works best when cutting shift housing, or the cutting wheel of an electric rotary tool works, too. Where appropriate, always use metal end caps (called ferrules) to protect the ends of the housings.

The plastic sheathing that runs through the housing can become crimped when you cut the housing. Trying to run the cable through the crimped end can damage the cable, so before trying to insert the cable, open the sheathing. A small, sharp object like a sharpened spoke should work.

Over time, moisture will still penetrate the housing, and strands can break down under the repeated stress of shifting. So change your bike's housing periodically, depending on how much you ride.

Shift housing was designed for cables that are 1.1 or 1.2mm in diameter. Brake cables are generally 1.6 or 1.8mm in diameter. In addition to the size differences, shift housing cannot withstand the pressures that come from braking. Don't try to use shift housing for brake cables.

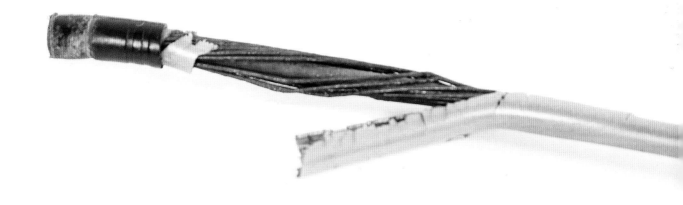

Shift Cable Maintenance

Cables live mostly outside the frame, exposed to the elements. Combine that with things like sweat and energy drinks, and cables can get sticky. This can be especially problematic for shift cables. For consistent shifting, the cables need to move smoothly within the housing.

There are some simple things you can do to maintain your cables before you have to replace them.

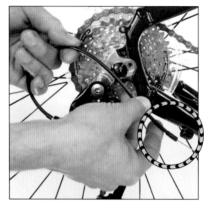

1 You need some slack in the cable. Shift your bike into the physically largest gear—the large chainring on the front derailleur and largest rear cog at the back. Stop moving the pedals and then move the shifter to the smallest chainring or the smallest rear cog. The chain shouldn't move, but you should have some slack in the cable.

2 Remove the cable housing from the rear cable stop.

3 Remove the cable housing from the rear barrel adjuster.

4 Move the housing to one side and apply a small amount of lube to the cable. Any bike-specific chain lube will work, but a dry lube won't attract as much dirt.

Pay special attention to the small piece of housing at the rear derailleur. Because of the bend in the housing, there can be additional friction in that spot.

Repeat the process with the housing at the front of the bike.

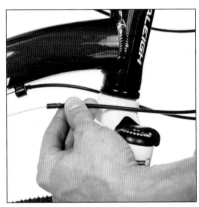

1 Remove the cable housing from the cable stop on the top tube, or down tube depending on how the cables are run on your particular bike.

2 Pull the cable housing away from the shifter so you can access the cable.

3 Lube the front cable as you did the rear cable.

When you're finished, put all the housings back in place. Then move the pedals forward to put tension back on the cable.

How often should you check your cables? It really depends on how much you ride. Some people never do it while more frequent riders do it once or twice a year.

Replacing Shift Cables

Over time, shift cables stretch and wear. One thing you can do to keep your bike working like new is to replace those cables.

To replace cables for dual-control or trigger shifters, the process is the same. The hardest part is figuring out how the cable feeds into your specific shifter. When you've figured out that part, the remaining steps are the same, regardless of the style of shifter you have on your bike.

One step that's the same with almost all shifters is shifting your bike so your chain is on the smallest rear cog before you start to remove the cable.

Replacing Dual-Control and Trigger Shifter Cables

To begin, clip the cable crimp end, loosen the derailleur anchor bolt, and start feeding the cable up through the shifter. In the case of a dual-control shifter, you might have to squeeze the brake lever to access the cable port.

1 Remove the shifter cover.

2 Insert the new cable into your shifter.

3 Feed the cable through the shifter and into the housing.

4 Insert the housing into the barrel adjuster.

5 Feed the cable in the housing through the first cable stop.

6 Most bikes have a cable guide on the bottom of the bottom bracket shell. Feed the cable through this guide, ensuring the cable is fully situated in the channels.

7 Feed the cable through the small piece of housing (in the case of a rear derailleur), and insert the housing into the rear cable stop.

8 Insert the cable through the barrel adjuster.

9 Feed through the anchor bolt.

10 Tighten the bolt and readjust the derailleur.

Replacing Twist Shifter Cables

On a twist shifter, the cable comes out easier if the bike is shifted to the smallest rear cog, but that isn't absolutely necessary.

1 If your twist shifter has a cover, remove it to get to the cable.

2 Insert the cable into the shifter.

3 Feed the cable through the shifter.

4 And pull the cable through.

5 Getting the cable end through the shifter might be tricky. You might need to use a small screwdriver to slightly pull back the grip.

After you've removed the old cable, reinsert the new cable into the shifter using the same steps outlined in the preceding section.

If you have a bike with internally routed cables, familiarize yourself with where the cable exits the frame before you remove the old cable. The steps for replacing the cables is the same, except you can't see the cables so you have to go more by feel.

Adjusting Rear Derailleurs

Few parts on your bike see as much action as the rear derailleur. The tight spacing and tolerances that give today's bikes such great performance mean small changes in cable tension can result in big changes in shifting performance. The proper adjustments can keep your rear derailleur shifting fast and smooth.

1 When adjusting the rear derailleur, shift the derailleur so the chain is on the smallest cog. The upper pulley should be in line with this cog. There should be no tension on the cable.

2 Look for the high- and low-limit screws, which are identified by the letters *H* and *L*.

3 If the cog and pulley are not in alignment, use the high-limit screw to move the pulley into the correct position.

If you're having trouble lining up the upper pulley with the smallest cog, be sure your derailleur hanger isn't bent.

4 To check the low-limit alignment, pedal the bike with one hand and push the derailleur so the chain sits on the largest cog.

5 If the upper pulley does not line up, adjust the low-limit screw.

6 Pull the shift cable taut, and tighten the anchor bolt.

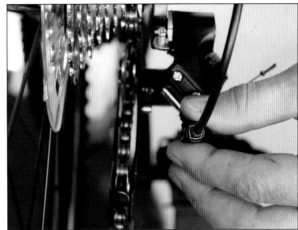

7 Pedal the bike and shift through the gears. Use the barrel adjuster to make fine tension changes to the cable, turning it in the direction you want the chain to go. If, for example, the chain needs to go up, turn the barrel adjuster counterclockwise.

Adjusting Front Derailleurs

For a piece of equipment that does relatively little, the front derailleur can cause a lot of frustration for home mechanics. It must be that there are so few places to actually make adjustments. But don't let that scare you. You can still successfully adjust your bike's front derailleur.

If the front derailleur starts to misbehave, the first thing many people do is start adjusting the limit screws. Resist this urge. In many cases, this just makes things worse.

Instead, first be sure the derailleur's outer cage is running parallel to the large chainring. If it isn't, loosen the derailleur and rotate it until it's in alignment.

Ideally, you want to set the limit screws with very little tension on the cable. This is especially true of the low-limit screw. If there's too much tension on the cable, you won't be able to make adjustments.

1 Start with the chain on the small chainring ...

2 ... and on the largest rear cog.

If the chain won't drop to the small chainring, leave a little more of a gap between the back derailleur plate and the chain.

3 Locate the high- and low-limit screws.

4 Set the low-limit screw so the back derailleur plate is nearly touching the chain.

At this point, it's good to have tension on the cable. So with the chain still on the small chainring, pull the cable taut, and tighten the anchor bolt.

5 To set the high-limit screw, move the chain to the large chainring and the smallest rear cog. You want as little clearance as possible between the chain and the derailleur cage. The derailleur should shift smoothly without rubbing.

6 After you've set the limit screws, you can make fine cable tension adjustments using the barrel adjuster.

Having the limit screws set too loose is where trouble often starts. That's when your chain will start dropping off the small chainring or fall off the large chainring. Ultimately, you want everything to be as close as it can be without rubbing or making noise.

Chapter 5

Freewheels and Cassettes

They're often overlooked, but both freewheels and cassettes are small parts that, if neglected, can cause you big problems on the road. But how do you tell one from the other? In this chapter, you learn the difference between freewheels and cassettes, as well as how to remove and install both. Finally, you discover easy ways you can extend the life of these very important components on your bike with some simple maintenance.

Freewheels Versus Cassettes

The very first bicycles had only one fixed gear. As long as the rear wheel was turning, the pedals and, therefore, your feet were moving as well. The invention of the freewheel gave the rider the capability to run multiple gears and coast on the bicycle.

The gears on the back of your bike are generically referred to as a cluster, but there are really two totally different systems—freewheels and cassettes.

cogs

ratcheting mechanism

A Look at Freewheels

With a freewheel, the ratcheting mechanism and the cogs are a single unit, and that unit threads onto the rear hub. The action of you pedaling tightens the freewheel. No tools are necessary for installation.

Freewheels are most widely available in five-, six-, or seven-speed configurations.

A Look at Cassettes

Most current bikes are equipped with a cassette hub. With a cassette hub, the ratcheting mechanism is a part of the hub. This splined "freehub" body accepts the cogs and spacers that make up the gear cluster. The cassette is held in place by a lock ring, and a lock ring tool is required for installation. Cassettes are available in 8, 9, 10, and 11 speeds.

In the 1980s and 1990s, cassettes could be taken apart and customized to some degree. However, most cassettes now are a single unit that's pinned together, and few bike shops sell individual cogs.

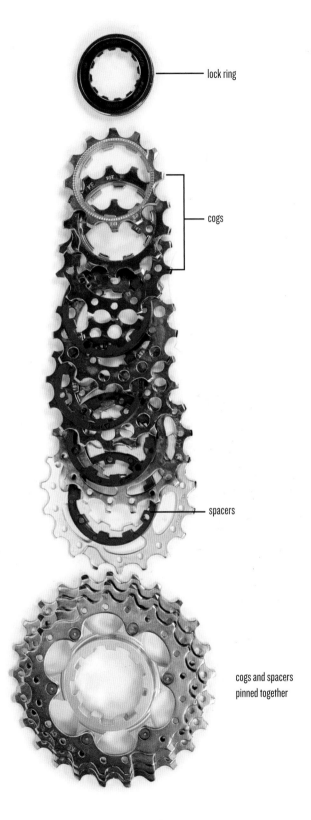

lock ring

cogs

spacers

cogs and spacers
pinned together

Lubricating Freewheels and Cassettes

Your bicycle is full of areas where metal contacts metal. In any of these places, a little lubrication is a good thing. But lube isn't needed everywhere, or in large amounts.

The cogs on your freewheel or cassette require no lubrication. Overlubing the chain, or applying lube directly to the cogs, attracts dirt and grime, which shortens the lifespan of the chain and ultimately the cluster itself.

However, some parts of the freewheel or cassette can, and should, be lubed.

If your freewheel is noisy, or if it's gotten sticky from years of use, you can lubricate it with oil. This process can take some time, and it's going to be easier (and cleaner) if you remove the freewheel from the hub.

1 Holding the freewheel with your hand, drip lube around the top ring of the freewheel.

2 Spin the freewheel until the oil works its way down through the seals. Repeat until the freewheel operates to your liking.

Freewheels are filled with dozens of very small bearings. It's best not to take them apart.

When installing a new cassette, it's a good idea to apply a light coating of grease to the freehub body. This practice is often debated in the bike world, but whenever you have two metal pieces coming together, a little lube isn't a bad thing.

The cassette's lock ring threads into the freehub body. Whenever you remove or replace a cassette, give these threads a small amount of grease as well.

Removing and Installing Freewheels

At one point, it wasn't uncommon to have freewheels in different sizes that all fit your bike. Then, you could choose which freewheel to use based on the terrain you were going to ride. Although the practice isn't as common these days, at some point, you will need to change or replace your freewheel.

Removing a Freewheel

To remove your freewheel, you're going to need the appropriate freewheel removal tool, a large wrench, or a vise. Most current freewheels use a spline based on the Shimano standard, but older freewheels could have a different-size spline or prongs. Verify which freewheel you have before you buy a tool.

> The old prong-style freewheel tools were prone to failure. If you're using one, it's good idea to secure the tool in the freewheel with your axle nut or skewer.

1 After you've removed the quick-release skewer or axle nuts, clamp your freewheel tool, if you're using one, in the vise.

2 Lower the wheel over the tool so the splines are aligned, and gently press down until the tool is fully inserted into the freewheel.

3 Using both hands, turn the entire wheel counterclockwise until the freewheel breaks free.

4 Continue turning until the freewheel is off the wheel. If the freewheel has been on the wheel for a long time, it might be a challenge to remove. Use consistent pressure, and it will eventually break free.

Installing a Freewheel

You can install your freewheel by hand. Apply a small amount of grease on the threads of the hub and thread the freewheel clockwise onto the hub. Take care not to cross-thread the freewheel on the hub. If the threads are properly aligned, the freewheel should turn easily by hand. If you feel resistance, stop, remove the freewheel, and start again.

If don't have a freewheel tool to finish the job, the force of your pedaling will complete the tightening.

If you don't have a vise, you can use a large adjustable wrench to remove the freewheel. Insert the freewheel removal tool into the freewheel, put your wrench on the tool, and turn counterclockwise until the freewheel breaks free. Then spin the freewheel tool by hand until the freewheel is off the wheel.

Removing and Installing Cassettes

Cassette hubs represent an improvement over freewheels in that they enable you to replace just the cogs, and not the whole unit. Because the cassette "freewheels" in the same direction the lock ring comes off, you need three tools to remove a cassette: a cassette lock ring tool, a chain whip, and a wrench.

Removing a Cassette

To remove a cassette, you must first remove the quick-release skewer or axle nuts.

1 Align the splines of the lock ring tool, and install it fully in the cassette. Notice that the tool spins freely counterclockwise. Placing the chain whip on the cassette keeps the cassette from moving. With a wrench, turn the lock ring tool in a counterclockwise direction.

2 Remove the lock ring, and you can now remove the cassette.

Installing a Cassette

The lock ring tool is the only tool you need to install a cassette.

1 Align the splines of the cassette with the splines on the freehub body.

2 Apply a small amount of grease to the threads of the lock ring.

3 By hand, begin to thread the lock ring into the freehub body.

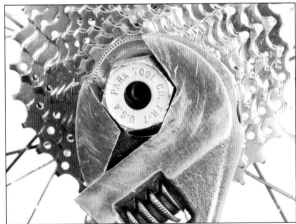

4 Insert the lock ring tool into the splines of the lock ring. With a wrench, turn the lock ring clockwise until it's fully tightened.

Recognizing Worn Cassette Bodies

Cassette bodies are generally durable, long lasting, and problem free. However, they're not infallible, and you should be aware of a few things when it comes to cassette bodies.

In an attempt to save weight, some manufacturers started using aluminum for their cassette bodies. The constant pressure on the rear wheel can "notch" these aluminum bodies. It might not present a problem when riding, but it does require a little more of your attention. Over time, and with constant pressure, the notching can make it nearly impossible to remove your cassette.

If you have a wheel with an aluminum cassette body, inspect it from time to time for wear. Remove the cassette, and look for notching on the body. Check the cassette lock ring periodically as well to ensure the cassette hasn't gotten loose.

If the cassette body has gotten worn, the notches in the splines can sometimes be filed smooth to prolong the cassette body's life. But if the cassette body becomes too worn, it must be replaced.

Regardless of the external material, some cassette body wear is internal. The majority of cassette bodies still use loose ball bearings, and when these wear out, it's easier and more cost effective to replace the whole unit.

It's uncommon, but cassette bodies can become loose. Manufacturers vary how they design cassette bodies, but many are affixed to the hub with a 10-millimeter Allen wrench. If yours is loose, give it a quick tighten with the wrench.

notched cassette body

unnotched cassette body

If your wheel has a cassette body made of steel, which is more durable and stronger than aluminum, wear is less of a concern.

Minimizing Wear and Tear

Anytime you have metal-on-metal contact, you're going to have wear. This is especially true for the components in your drivetrain. Chains, chainrings, and cogs are in a perpetual state of motion and, therefore, are wearing all the time. But with some very simple tasks, you can minimize this wear and prolong the life of your drivetrain.

Cleanliness

The best thing you can do to lengthen the life of your drivetrain is keep it clean. Nothing wears out parts on a bike faster than dirt. Dirt and road grime gets in between the chain and sprockets and grinds away at both in a vicious cycle. Taking the time to clean your bike not only prolongs its life, but also makes your bike shift better and quieter.

You don't have to get out a bucket and soapy water every week to keep things clean. Just the simple act of wiping down the chain and rear derailleur with a clean rag helps.

Lubricant Use

The biggest contributor to a dirty drivetrain is too much lubricant. Excess lube on the outside of the chain transfers to the cassette cogs and chainrings, and makes them magnets for dirt.

What lubricant you use on your chain is important as well. You should only use a bicycle-specific chain lube on your chain—not motor oil, three-in-one oil, sewing machine oil, axle grease, or anything else. Bicycle-specific lube is lightweight and designed for your chain. Anything else is just too heavy.

Too much lube is worse than none at all. Use it sparingly.

Riding Style

How you ride also has an effect on drivetrain wear. As bikes have added more and more gears, chains have gotten narrower. If you "spin," this isn't really much of an issue. Riders who tend to "mash" their pedals, on the other hand, wear out chains much faster.

This isn't to say you should change your riding style. Rather, if you have a tendency to push bigger gears, you should watch for drivetrain wear much more closely. Riding on a worn-out chain wears not only the chain, but also cassette, and in extreme cases, the chainrings as well.

Wheel Care

Wipe down the braking surface of your rims, and check your brake pads periodically, too. Brake pads can pick up small fragments of aluminum from your rims, and dust and dirt from the rims can get ground into your rims while you brake.

Unchecked, both of these things can shorten the lifespan of your wheels.

The Differences in Chain Wrap

When people talk about *chain wrap*, they can be talking about one of two things.

Chain Wrap Adjustment

The most common use of the term refers to the *chain wrap adjustment* of your rear derailleur. Controlled by a small screw at the back of the rear derailleur, this "B tension" screw adjusts the amount of tension on the upper pulley as well as the amount of chain that wraps around the rear cogs.

Always make a chain wrap adjustment with your bike in the lowest, easiest, gear.

Loosen the screw to move the pulley closer, and tighten the screw to move the pulley away. When the upper pulley is closer to the largest cog, you have better shifting. Noise and shifting problems can arise when the pulley gets too close and hits the biggest cog.

Chain Wrap Capacity

The second explanation of chain wrap is the *capacity* of a specific derailleur and gearing combination. Not all rear derailleurs accept all cassettes. For example, a standard "short-cage" road bike derailleur generally has the capacity for a largest rear cog with 27 teeth. Anything larger requires a smaller rear cassette or a different rear derailleur.

Say you really like your bike, and don't want to get a new one, but you want a larger rear cassette for climbing. Before you go out and buy a new cassette, be sure your current derailleur has the capacity for the larger cogs.

To determine your chain wrap capacity, you need to count the teeth on your chainrings and the number of teeth on your smallest and largest cassette cogs. Subtract the number of teeth on the smallest chainring from the number of teeth on the largest chainring. Then subtract the number of teeth on your smallest rear cog from the number of teeth on your largest rear cog. Add the two numbers, and you get your bike's chain wrap capacity. Here's the formula:

chain wrap capacity = (large chainring – small chainring) + (largest rear cog – smallest rear cog)

So if you have chainring sizes of 50 and 34 teeth, and you want to run a cassette with a range of 12 to 32, here's how you'd calculate your chain wrap capacity:

chain wrap capacity = (50 – 34) + (32 – 12)

= 16 + 20

= 36

Therefore, you need a rear derailleur that has a chain wrap capacity of 36.

Chain wrap capacities vary from derailleur to derailleur, so refer to the component manufacturer for specifics.

Chapter 6
Chains

Even though it's been around for more than 100 years, the bicycle chain is still the most efficient and affordable way to drive a bike. Proper chain maintenance can prolong the life of your components and ensure your bike is road ready whenever you are. In this chapter, you discover how to tell when it's time for a new chain, learn the steps for proper lubrication and chain replacement, and get tips on cleaning your chain to prolong its life.

Understanding Chain Differences

Bike chains come in different sizes, and the size of your chain is determined by two factors: pitch and width. Pitch is the distance between the chain's pins, and width is the distance between the chain's inner plates.

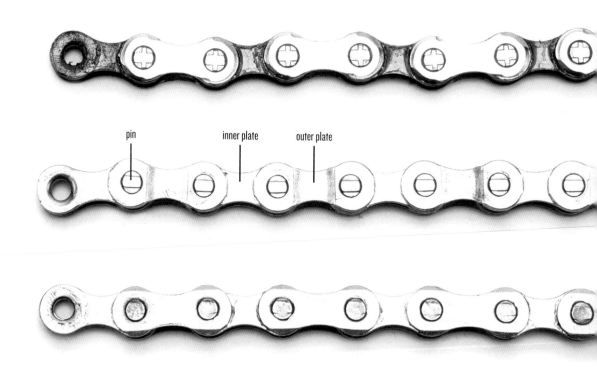

pin   inner plate   outer plate

The chain pitch on all modern bikes is $^1/_2$ inch (12.5mm), but the width of the chain varies depending on the type of bicycle. On a single-speed bike, or a bike with an internally geared hub, the width of the chain is $^1/_8$ inch (3.2mm). The width of the chain on a geared derailleur bike is generally $^3/_{32}$ inch (2.5mm).

For derailleur bikes, you also need to consider the number of rear sprockets a chain can support. Your rear hub lives in a fixed amount of space, and that space has not gotten any larger, even as the number of gears has grown. To accommodate more gears, the space between the cogs has narrowed, and the plates of the chain have been made thinner. If your chain is too wide or too narrow, you won't be able to shift correctly. When replacing your chain, check that your new chain is designed to support the number of gears on your bike.

Once you've determined you have the correct chain, you need to consider how the chain is attached. When bikes only had six or seven rear gears, you could just push one pin most of the way out and break the chain. To reinstall, you simply pushed that pin back into the chain. With current chains, this isn't an option.

Many chains now use a connecting link, a special link you can use to join the chain without the need for any tools. These links can make connecting and disconnecting easier when it comes time to clean or replace your chain. Some connecting links are reusable and some aren't, so be sure to know which you have before disconnecting your chain.

Not all chain manufacturers use the same method to connect the chain. For example, Shimano chains use a special connecting pin. These pins, once used, cannot be pushed out and reused. Moreover, Shimano actually has a chain that must be installed to run in a specific direction.

You need to replace and clean your chain from time to time. Knowing what kind of chain you need, and how you're going to connect it, makes the job much faster and easier.

The "master link" used on single-speed bikes isn't the same as the connecting links used on derailleur bikes. The two are not interchangeable.

Cleaning a Chain

Cleaning your bike chain is a mundane task many people often neglect to do—or don't do at all. However, it's an important part of bike maintenance that extends the life of your chain and improves your bike's performance.

The most thorough way to clean your chain is to remove it from the bike. You can use any container, such as an old coffee can, but an old bicycle water bottle works best. Pour in some chain cleaner, add the chain, close the lid securely, and shake. Remove the chain from the bottle, wipe it off well, and allow it to dry.

If your chain uses special pins or connecting links that aren't reusable, you might be reluctant to remove your chain for cleaning. Fortunately, you can clean your chain without removing it from your bike. It's messy and unglamorous, but it needs to be done.

One way to clean your chain when it's still on your bike is by using a chain-cleaning device that attaches to the chain.

You fill the small plastic box with solvent, fit it around the chain, and back pedal the bike as brushes inside the box scrub the chain clean. It works very well, but you'll probably get some solvent on the floor. When you're done, wipe off the chain (and anything else covered in solvent), give it some time to dry, and lubricate the chain.

To clean your chain the low-tech way, just grab a rag and some chain cleaner. Spray on the cleaner, let it sit for a minute, and wipe it off. It's not as thorough, but it works.

When manually cleaning your chain while it's still on your bike, be sure to carefully wipe off any overspray that hits the bike. Also, keep the solvent away from bearing areas like the hubs or the bottom bracket.

Lubricating a Chain

How often should you lubricate your chain? There's no hard-and-fast answer. It depends more on how often you ride, where you ride, and the type of lubricant you use.

Many riders overestimate the amount of lubricant they need, but too much lube can be more damaging to a chain than too little. If you can run your finger over the chain and nothing comes off, you should apply some lube. Also apply lube if your drivetrain starts squeaking.

When purchasing a lubricant, select one designed specifically for bicycle chains. Other lubes and oils are too heavy and will attract too much dirt. Lubricant is often sold in drip bottles or aerosol cans. Using a drip bottle takes a bit more time but wastes less lube and makes less of a mess.

Original WD-40 has many uses, but it's not a lubricant. It's a penetrating solvent, and it should not be used on bike chains.

Start by finding a spot on your chain you can find again. If your chain has a connecting link, for example, this is a great spot to begin with. If you have a Shimano chain, start at the pin used to connect the chain. It usually looks different from the rest.

With a drip bottle, apply one drop of lube on every pin. The lube only needs to be down inside the chain's plates and rollers. Lube on the outside of your chain doesn't really do anything but attract dirt. Work your way around the chain until you reach the link you started with.

If you use an aerosol, opt for a dry lube. Spray the lube at the back of the bike, being careful not to get lube on the brake pads or the braking surface of your rims.

When you've finished, use a clean rag to wipe off any excess lube.

Replacing a Chain

Replacing your bike's chain is a similar task to changing the oil in your car—basic and necessary maintenance you might not always *want* to do but you *need* to do to keep your vehicle on the road. Caring for your chain before it wears out extends the life of your bike and helps prevent unexpected breakdowns.

Stretched Chains

As you ride, the pressure applied to your pedals begins to stretch your chain. The rate it stretches depends on a variety of factors, including where you ride, your riding style, dirt, weather, and excess lube.

Unfortunately, you might not be aware of your chain stretching. Often the first sign of a chain problem is when you begin to have difficulty shifting. If you've reached this point, you need to replace the chain—and you might have to replace more than just the chain.

As a chain wears, the cassette cog teeth also wear. When you install a new chain, it might not mesh with the worn cogs, and shifting might be more problematic than it was with the old chain. The only option at this point is to replace the chain and the cassette. In very extreme cases, you might have to replace one or more of the chainrings as well.

To avoid reaching this point, you need to check your chain often for stretching. Some people suggest you check chain length with a tape measure, but that's not an entirely accurate method.

Stretch isn't the only reason to install a new chain. You also need to replace your chain if it's become twisted or if you notice cracked plates, several stiff links, or an abundance of rust. And if a chain breaks during a ride, replace it when you get home.

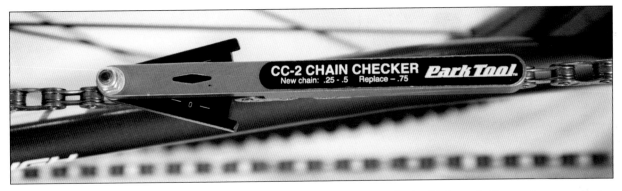

A chain checker is a better, more accurate way to measure your chain. This tool clips onto your chain and measures the distance between the chain's pins.

Replacing Your Chain

You only need a couple things to replace your chain: a new chain and a chain tool. Chains are designed to fit all bikes and, therefore, only come in one length. They also come with a connecting link, or pin, and everything you need to install the chain. You will, more than likely, have to use your chain tool to shorten the new chain to fit your specific bike. A chain tool supports the chain's outer plates and uses a slightly smaller pin to install or remove the pin in a link of chain.

1 Remove the old chain. If your old chain doesn't have a connecting link, use your chain tool to remove a pin and break the chain.

2 If you have a connecting link, you might be able to separate the chain by hand. Grab the links on either side of the connecting link and squeeze together to unhook the connecting link.

You can also use pliers specifically made for use with chains to remove the connecting link. Place the plier jaws on either side of the connecting link, and squeeze to disengage the connecting link.

When the chain is broken, pull it through the derailleur cage plates and remove it from your bike.

3 To install a new chain, feed it through the front derailleur, placing it on the largest chainring ...

4 ... around the smallest rear cog ...

5 ... through the pulleys of
the rear derailleur ...

6 ... and bring it back
toward the front of the
bike.

Shortening Your Chain

You'll likely need to shorten your chain before connecting it. To determine the correct length of the new chain, be sure the chain is on the large chainring in front and the smallest rear cog. Pull the two ends of the chain together until the derailleur cage plate is perpendicular to the ground. The excess chain is the amount to cut off. Use your chain tool to cut the chain to the correct length.

1 To reconnect the new chain, install the connecting link and line up the two pieces ...

2 ... and pull tight to secure.

Correcting Chain Problems

Because they're relatively problem-free, chains are sometimes overlooked when diagnosing bike issues. However, if you're having trouble shifting, the chain may be the culprit.

Rusty Chain

One obvious chain problem is rust. If your chain is covered in rust, it's not going to work properly. You usually can remove a little bit of surface rust with a good cleaning and a dose of lubricant. If your chain is so rusty the links don't move, it's time to get a new one.

Stiff Link

If your bike isn't shifting quite right and the rear derailleur clicks or jumps every pedal revolution or two, your chain might have a stiff link.

A stiff link occurs when the inner and outer plates of the chain push too tightly against each other. If you back pedal the bike and watch the rear derailleur, you should be able to spot the problem link easily. When you've found the link, it's relatively easy to repair.

Place your thumbs on the stiff link, and with your hands, work the chain back and forth. You might need to repeat this process a few times to loosen the link.

Twisted Chain

A more serious problem is a twisted chain. This often happens when you're making a hard shift. The chain gets hung up on the front derailleur during the shift, and if you keep the power on the pedals or try to just pedal through the hang-up, the chain can become twisted.

You can also twist your chain if the low limit screw of your rear derailleur is too loose. This can cause the chain to shift into the rear wheel. This is a serious issue that generally results in not only a twisted chain, but also a ruined rear derailleur, derailleur hanger, and possible rear wheel.

Any time the chain is twisted, the only option is to replace the whole chain.

When a Chain Falls Off

It's not uncommon for bike chains to fall off either the biggest or smallest chainring while you're riding. Sometimes the cause is a front derailleur that's slightly out of adjustment, and sometimes it just happens for no real reason.

If your chain falls off while you're in motion, don't panic. Get off your bike, and move away from traffic. There's an easy way to fix this, and you shouldn't even get that dirty.

When you're off the road, push the cage of the rear derailleur forward.

This provides the necessary slack in the chain so you can lift the chain back up onto the chainring.

When you've replaced your chain, spin the pedals a few rounds to be sure everything is back in place correctly.

If your chain falls off repeatedly, you might want to check the adjustment of your derailleur.

Although it's possible for the chain to come off the rear cassette during a shift, it's almost always an adjustment or derailleur hanger issue.

It might be possible to shift the chain back onto the chainrings. This is something that must be done very gently. It's tricky to do, so it's better to stop your bike and replace the chain by hand.

Chapter 7

Hubs

They might be small, but hubs play a big role in your bike's performance. Loose hubs can damage wheels, while overly tight hubs can result in unnecessary drag. In this chapter, you learn how to identify what kind of hub your bike has and adjust it for optimum performance. You also get an in-depth look at internally geared hubs.

The Anatomy of a Hub

The hub sits in the middle of the wheel and makes it possible for the wheel to rotate. Different hubs vary in quality, but they all have basically the same parts for both front and rear wheels. A good hub spins freely, needs little attention, and lasts for a very long time.

The body of the hub, or *shell,* includes the *flange,* which holds one end of the spokes, and the *race,* which holds the bearings inside the shell. The axle goes through the middle of the shell, and threaded onto the axle are the *cone* and *lock nut.* The *bearings* spin between the race and the cone, the cone controls the hub adjustment, and the lock nut holds the adjustment. Lastly, the *dust cover* keeps dirt and grime from getting inside the hub.

Hub adjustment refers to the amount of load the cone places on the hub bearing. The correct amount of load takes out any side-to-side play and allows the hub bearing to spin freely. The lock nut tightens down against the cone to prevent it from loosening.

Sealed-Bearing Versus Loose-Ball Hubs

Bicycle hubs are available with either sealed or loose ball bearings situated between the race and the cone. Both types have benefits, and fine choices are available in both versions. Let's look at the characteristics of each of these hubs.

The series of seals found in a sealed-bearing hub generally makes them better in wet weather. If you live in a wet climate, or use your bike mainly for transportation, this setup could save you hours of maintenance.

Sealed-Bearing Hubs

As the name implies, in sealed-bearing hubs, the ball bearings that enable the wheel to spin are sealed within the hub, between the race and the cone, and are not visible from the outside. Due to this construction, a sealed-bearing hub is often stronger and more durable than a loose-ball hub.

However, the hub is one of the main areas where your bike can encounter friction, and in lower-quality sealed-bearing hubs, you have the chance for more drag. Also, because sealed bearings are preadjusted, most sealed-bearing hubs are not adjustable. However, a few hubs on the market include a preload adjustment, or the capability to take out any play in the axle with a greater degree of control.

For the novice home mechanic, the sealed-bearing hub's lack of serviceability could be viewed as a benefit. When the hub bearing becomes worn, you can simply replace the bearing rather than worry about adjusting it.

Loose-Ball Hubs

Loose-ball hubs have been used in bicycles for many years. Serious cyclists appreciate the ability to make adjustments easily to these hubs, such as replacing grease with oil to reduce friction before a race.

Ease of adjustment can also help mitigate some of the problems caused by small imperfections in other components. Bicycle parts, regardless of cost, are imperfect things. This is especially true of the parts found in low- to midrange bikes. Loose-ball hubs are much more tolerant of these imperfections, and they make it easier to achieve proper adjustment and function.

However, because the bearings are not as protected, more maintenance is required with a loose-ball hub. If you ride a lot, an annual hub overhaul is advisable to keep them rolling smoothly.

Two of the oldest and largest component manufacturers, Shimano and Campagnolo, still offer only loose-ball hubs.

Adjusting Loose-Ball Hubs

When a hub is correctly adjusted, it should spin as freely as possible with no friction or play. A hub that's too loose has excess play even when the wheel is on the bike. A hub that's too loose doesn't spin freely.

Adjusting your loose-ball hubs requires at least one, and preferably two, cone wrenches. These small, thin wrenches come in many different sizes, and some versions have two sizes per wrench. Having two of each size wrench is ideal but not required. You also need an open-end or adjustable wrench for the lock nut. It isn't absolutely necessary, but using a vise makes the adjustment considerably easier.

Adjusting a Front Wheel Hub

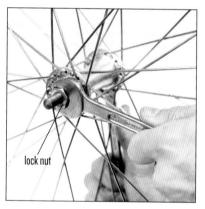

1 First, remove the rubber dust covers, if your hub has them, on each side. Pinch them between your thumb and forefinger, and lift them off. Removing the covers exposes the cones.

2 If the hub is too tight, place a cone wrench on each cone, and turn them counterclockwise. This loosens the cones while tightening them against the lock nuts.

3 If the hub is loose, try tightening the lock nuts. It's possible that tightening the lock nuts will take the play out of the axle.

If the hub is still loose, loosen the lock nut on one side of the hub. Slightly tighten the cone on the same side, and retighten the lock nut. Check the adjustment of the hub by turning the axle and attempting to move it side to side by hand.

Adjusting a Rear Wheel Hub

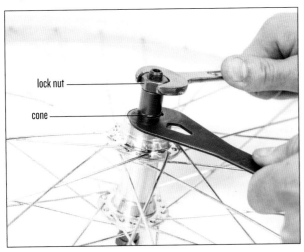

To adjust the rear hub, first remove the freewheel. Once the freewheel has been removed, the adjustment is the same as the front wheel. The cones, however, are a different size and require a different wrench, so check to see what your bike needs.

With a cassette hub, even with the cogs removed, the cones on the drive side generally aren't within reach. Checking the adjustment on the drive side requires loosening the lock nut and cone on the *nondrive* side. This enables you to move the axle outward on the drive side enough to check the adjustment. Because this is a somewhat difficult process, most of the time, adjusting a cassette rear hub is done only on the nondrive side.

Before making the adjustment on the nondrive side, you might want to check that the cone and lock nut are properly counterlocked on the drive side. This can be tricky, but it ensures that you adjust your hub correctly.

It takes some practice to get the feel for a properly adjusted hub, so be patient with yourself as you learn. Don't worry if it takes a lot of trial and error to get your hubs properly adjusted. Sometimes the key to being successful is knowing when to *stop* making adjustments.

Measuring Rear Hub Spacing

It's not unusual to want to add new components to your bike, and wheels are a very common upgrade. When adding new wheels to your bike, you have to be aware of the rear hub spacing.

Rear hub spacing is the distance between the inside edges of the dropouts. This measurement needs to pretty closely match the distance between the outside edges of the lock nuts on the hub of the new wheel you're thinking of putting on your bike.

Hubs are measured using what's called *over locknut dimension,* or O.L.D. If you have a set of calipers, you can measure the distance between your hub's lock nuts (outside to outside). Or you can measure the distance between the dropouts in your frame with a tape measure.

Although the two distances should match, a small amount of variance is acceptable. For example, some manufactures build their frames with 132.5-millimeter rear spacing. This enables you to use either 130- or 135-millimeter rear hubs. Typically, road bikes use 130 millimeter spacing and mountain bikes use 135 millimeter.

With new bikes and new wheels, determining the rear hub spacing is seldom a problem. However, if you're trying to add new wheels to an older bike, you might have a problem. Older road bikes, for example, could have 126-millimeter spacing. A newer 130-millimeter hub wouldn't fit this bike.

For at least the last two decades, front hub spacing has been 100 millimeters on most bikes, so determining the front hub spacing isn't nearly as important as doing so for the rear hub.

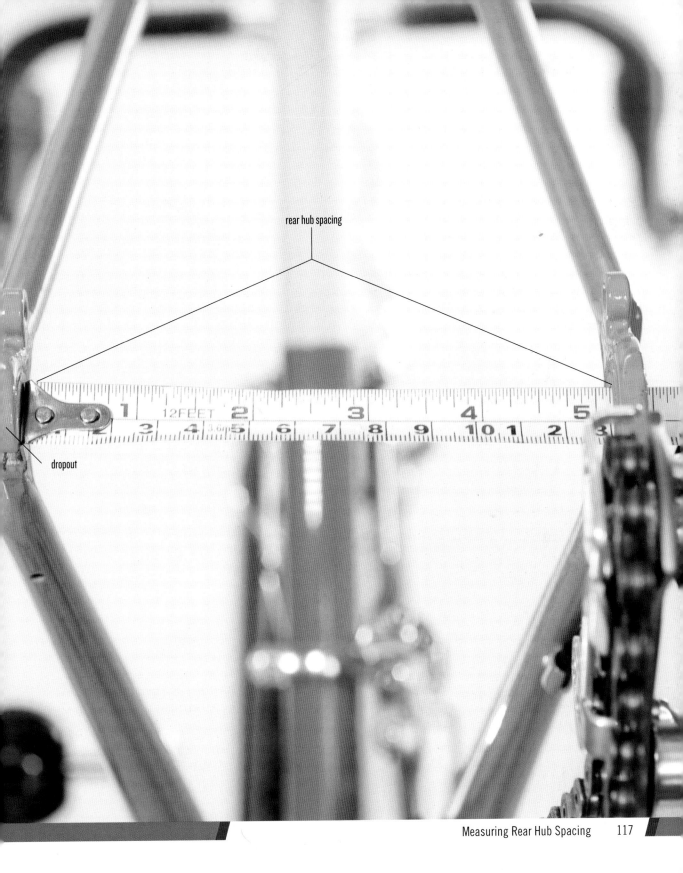

rear hub spacing

dropout

Internally Geared Hubs

On some bikes, the mechanism responsible for shifting gears, called an *internally geared hub,* or *IGH,* is located within the rear hub. IGHs first became popular with old English 3-speed bikes and have remained popular because of their simplicity and ease of use.

IGHs are very robust, which has made them a favorite of riders who use their bikes for transportation. Because the gearing system is enclosed within the hub, IGHs are relatively impervious to wet weather and dirt. Chain wear is minimized thanks to the single cog on the rear wheel, and being able to shift while stopped or coasting makes them very convenient for commuting in city traffic.

In most cases, the number of gears you can have with an IGH is limited. The most common IGHs have 3, 7, 8, or 11 gears. One model has up to 14 gears, and another claims an infinite number of ratios, but neither are very common.

Most riders focus on the benefits of these hubs, but few consider the inconveniences compared to a bike with a derailleur system. With an IGH, you lose the ability to have a quick-release rear wheel. This means a flat tire while riding requires more time and effort to repair. Also, you must carry a wrench to remove the wheel with an IGH. In addition, there's the matter of disconnecting the shift cable. Unlike on a derailleur bike, you must remove the shift cable from your IGH to remove the rear wheel. Especially if you use your bike very frequently, such as for transportation, these are important points to keep in mind.

Many people believe IGH systems are maintenance free. They might require less service than a derailleur system, but they do require some maintenance. Manufacturers generally recommend disassembling IGHs for cleaning and lubrication either annually or after a specific number of miles.

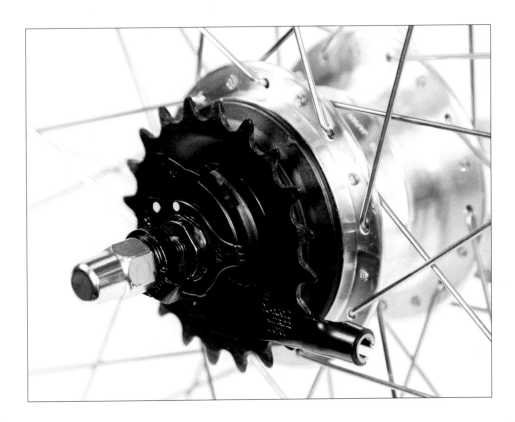

Wheels with Internally Geared Hubs

Removing and replacing wheels with internally geared hubs (IGHs) takes some special care. If you have a flat tire, for example, you can't just remove and replace the wheel if it has an IGH. There are unique steps you must take when working with wheels with IGHs.

Removing and replacing a wheel with an IGH sometimes requires gear adjustment, so the tasks are best done together.

Many different hubs are available, but in this section, we focus on two of the most common, the Shimano Nexus three speed and the Shimano Nexus seven speed.

On older internally geared hubs, you have to adjust the shifting every time you move the wheel. On newer hubs, this is no longer necessary.

The Shimano Nexus Three Speed

First, let's look at how to remove a wheel that has an IGH.

Removing a Wheel with a Shimano Nexus Three Speed Hub

1 If your hub has an external gearbox, disconnect it. Using an Allen wrench, loosen the bolt at the back of the gearbox, and remove the gearbox from the hub. Leave the cable connected to the gearbox.

2 Locate the push rod in the hub. Remove the push rod and set it aside. You can now loosen the axle nuts and remove your wheel.

Reinstalling a Wheel with a Shimano Nexus Three Speed Hub

1 Place the chain on the rear cog, and pull the axle into the dropout.

2 Tighten the axle nuts to secure the wheel.

3 Most every chain has what's called a "tight spot." This is an area where, because of small imperfections in the drivetrain components, the chain doesn't have any, or as much, slack. With the wheel secure in the dropout, turn the pedal with one hand and push up on the chain with your finger to locate the tight spot. When you find it, loosen the axle nuts and retighten the wheel in that spot.

4 Reinstall the push rod.

5 Reattach the gearbox, and tighten the bolt.

Adjusting the Shimano Nexus Three Speed Hub

1 Put your bike in second gear, and look at the gearbox window. The wide yellow bar should sit between the two thin yellow lines. If it doesn't, you need to make some adjustments.

2 To adjust the hub, loosen the lock nut and adjust the cable tension with the barrel adjuster until the wide yellow bar is evenly between the thin yellow lines.

The Shimano Nexus Seven Speed

The second type of hub doesn't have a gearbox. Instead, the cable connects directly to the hub.

Removing a Wheel with a Shimano Nexus Seven Speed Hub

1 To remove the wheel, pull forward on the shift cable housing to remove the housing from the cable stop.

2 With the provided slack, you should be able to remove the anchor bolt and free the shift cable.

3 At this point, you can loosen the axle nuts and remove your wheel.

Reinstalling a Wheel with a Shimano Nexus Seven Speed Hub

When it's time to reinstall the wheel, place the chain on the rear cog, pull the axle into the dropout, and tighten the axle nuts. Then reinsert the cable anchor and seat cable housing into the cable stop.

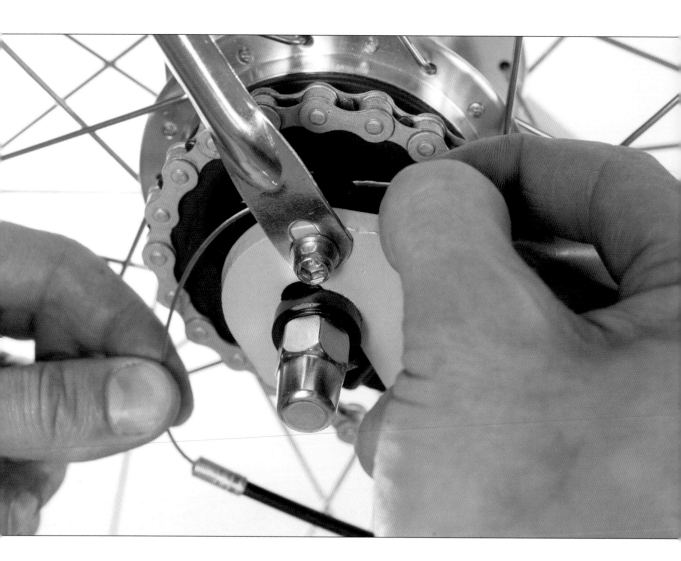

Adjusting the Shimano Nexus Seven Speed Hub

1   With this style hub, you check the adjustment in fourth gear. When the hub is properly adjusted, the red lines are aligned.

2   If necessary, use the barrel adjuster to fine-tune the cable tension until the red lines match up.

Checking for Play or Bent Axles

The easiest way to deal with a hub issue is to catch it early. If you continue to ride on a problem hub, it can quickly go from a small adjustment to a major problem.

One way to identify a loose hub is by listening to your bike. A loose hub sometimes makes a popping noise, especially when you're pedaling out of the saddle, or when standing up.

The easiest way to check for play, or movement, is when the wheel is still in the frame. If the wheel moves when it's tight in the frame, the hub is probably the problem. Grab the wheel and move it from side to side. In extreme cases, you can actually see the hub move around the axle.

Bent axes are tough to diagnose while the wheel is in the bike, and can be mistaken for a hub that's out of adjustment. It's not until you remove the wheel that the bent axle is noticeable.

With the wheel out of the bike, grab the axle with your fingers and try to move it. If there's play in the axle, you can adjust it. Left unattended, a bent axle can ruin the inside of your hub.

Solid axles are more likely to become bent than quick-release axles. But it is possible to bend a quick-release axle. When this happens, the skewer is most likely bent as well. A bent skewer can sometimes be straightened enough to be reused. A bent axle, however, must be replaced.

Chapter 8

Saddles and Seatposts

The saddle, or seat, is one of the most personal components on your bike. If you've ever ridden a bike with a saddle that wasn't quite right for you, you understand just how much that one part can affect your entire riding experience. In this chapter, you learn what to look for in a saddle, how to change and adjust your saddle, and how to determine your correct saddle height. Plus, you get some tips that might help make you more comfortable on your bike.

Types of Saddles

The main job of your bike's saddle, or seat, is to support your *ischial tuberosities,* or sit bones. The saddle needs to be wide enough to support those bones but not so wide that it causes chafing or other discomfort. Most saddles are plastic, covered in vinyl, with a layer of foam in between.

When you find your saddle uncomfortable, often your first thought is to find a softer one. But that's not always the right choice. When you sit on a softer saddle, your sit bones sink in, and the soft tissue can experience more pressure.

Most saddles today come with some sort of "comfort guarantee." Don't hesitate to try different models until you find the one that's just right for you.

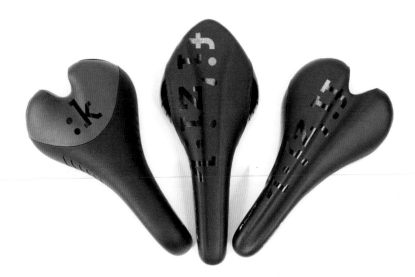

Racing Saddles

Racing-style bikes generally have saddles that are narrow and firm. They merely provide a "perch" for your sit bones. These saddles work best when the handlebar is level with or lower than the saddle.

 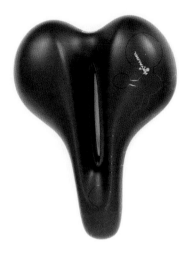

Comfort Saddles

As the handlebar rises, the saddle needs to support more of your weight. In these cases, a slightly wider saddle might be necessary. Such higher handlebar positions are often found on hybrid or comfort bikes.

Cut-Out Saddles

What about cut-out saddles? Many people love them, but just as many people don't.

The idea behind cut-out saddles is that the cut-out in the center of the saddle alleviates any soft tissue pressure by simply removing the saddle from that area. However, some riders find the perimeter of the cut-out actually applies pressure.

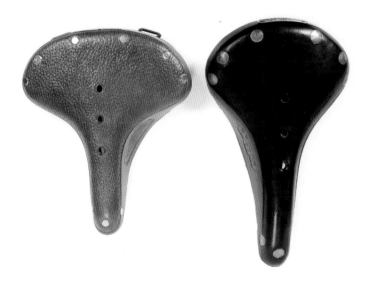

Leather Saddles

Leather saddles, prevalent in the 1970s, are making a bit of a comeback. Leather saddles are supportive, and over time, they conform to your body. They do take some time to break in, and they also require more care than a plastic saddle to ensure the leather stays soft and doesn't crack. A high percentage of long-distance touring riders still use leather saddles.

Adjusting Your Saddle

Saddle adjustment can drastically increase your comfort while you're on your bike. All seatposts can be adjusted fore and aft, or front and back. You can change the tilt of your saddle as well.

If, when you're riding your bike, you feel like you continually have to scoot back on the saddle, move it forward. If you're constantly moving forward on your seat, move it back. It's really that simple.

Make these changes in *millimeters* and only adjust one thing at a time. It only takes a small change to make a big difference. You want to be able to track the result of any adjustments you make, and if you change more than one thing at a time—up, down, forward, back, etc.—you won't know what move made the difference.

Whenever you change your saddle position, it's a good idea to mark the rails where the saddle was before you make the change. That way, if the adjustment doesn't work out, you can go back to where you started.

Types of Seatposts

Different seatposts have different types of clamps that hold the saddle in place, but the most common is the single-bolt clamp. This clamp lets you adjust the fore/aft and the tilt with one bolt.

On some lower-priced seatposts, the part of the clamp that holds the saddle rails is knurled to allow for micro adjustments. Failure to fully tighten this type of post results in the knurling being worn down. When that happens, the saddle won't stay in place, and you'll have to replace the seatpost.

A two-bolt post works similarly, except the tilt is set by tightening the two bolts individually.

single-bolt clamp

two-bolt post

Adjusting Your Saddle

1 Loosen both bolts to move the saddle fore and aft. As you tighten the bolts, you can see the tilt of the saddle change.

2 Overtightening the front bolt makes the nose of the saddle dip too low.

3 To avoid this, tighten the bolts slowly. Snug one and then the other until both bolts are fully tightened. This ensures the saddle stays level while you tighten the bolts.

Parts with threads need some grease from time to time. Don't be afraid to remove the bolts from your seatpost every year or so and apply some grease. It makes adjustments easier, and it might just take care of some the creaks your bike has been making.

On one type of single-bolt post, the bolt is on the side of the clamp. This is a very easy type of clamp to operate. By loosening the bolt, you can adjust the fore/aft and tilt. Simply loosen the bolt, adjust your saddle, and retighten the bolt.

Changing Saddles

If you're unhappy with the saddle you currently have, changing it is an easy and straightforward task. Maybe you have a saddle you really like, and you want to move it to a new bike. Or maybe your old saddle was damaged in a crash, or maybe it's just past its prime. Whatever the reason, it's easy to change saddles.

Before removing your old saddle, take note of the angle at which it sits. Take a measurement so you can duplicate your old saddle's position with the new one. Measuring from the nose of the saddle to some point on the stem or bar gives you a reference for where to place the new saddle. Remember, no two saddles are exactly the same, and differences in saddle lengths or saddle rails will affect your position from one saddle to the next.

Removing a Saddle from a Two-Bolt Seatpost

On a two-bolt seatpost, you may have to remove one of the bolts in order to remove the saddle. With one bolt removed and one loose, you will be able to move the top plate of the clamp enough to remove the saddle. Past that, the process is very similar to a single-bolt seatpost.

Removing a Saddle from a Single-Bolt Seatpost

Removing a single-bolt seatpost saddle is simple.

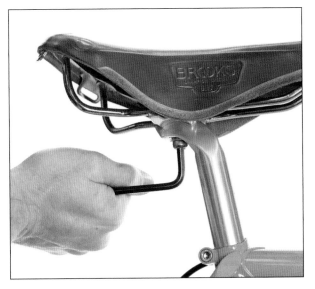

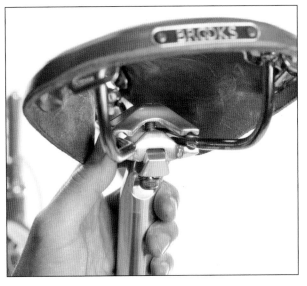

1 To change a saddle on a single-bolt seatpost, first loosen the bolt.

2 Rotate the top plate until it's perpendicular with the bottom plate.

3 Remove your saddle from the seatpost.

Then install the new saddle, and reverse the process to tighten it.

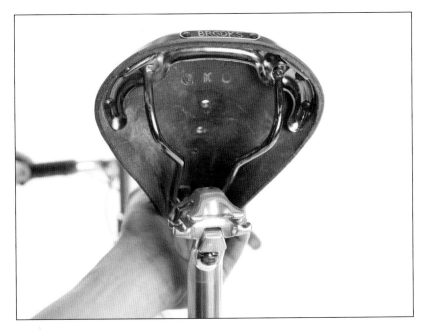

Removing a Saddle from a Straight Seatpost

If you're using a straight post, saddle swaps take a bit more work. You need to remove the saddle clamp and reinstall it on the new saddle.

1 Loosen both nuts on the sides of the saddle clamp and remove the saddle from the post.

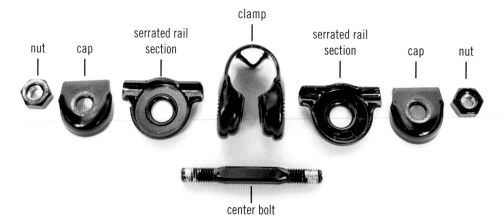

nut   cap   serrated rail section   clamp   serrated rail section   cap   nut

center bolt

2 Remove both nuts and take them out of the clamp. Remove the center bolt and the rest of the clamp from the saddle. Pay attention to the order all the pieces go together.

3 Place the center section of the clamp and one serrated rail section on the rail of the new saddle at about a 45-degree angle.

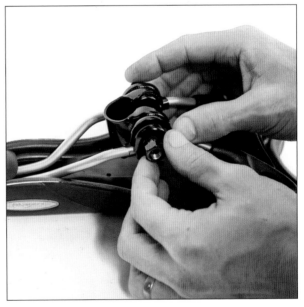

4 Place the other serrated rail section on the opposite saddle rail, and rotate the three pieces together down until they fit snugly between the two rails.

5 Assemble the rest of the clamp and attach the saddle to your seatpost.

Seatpost Sizes and Types

A seatpost seems like such a simple thing—a post with a clamp at the top that holds your saddle. But it has a very important job: it supports you.

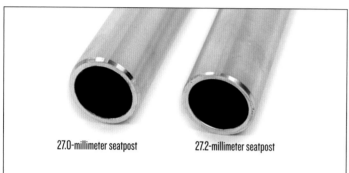

27.0-millimeter seatpost   27.2-millimeter seatpost

Seatposts come in a multitude of sizes, generally with a different size every $^2/_{10}$ of 1 millimeter. The tolerance between the frame and the seatpost must be that close to support your weight as you ride your bike.

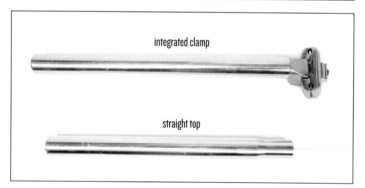

integrated clamp

straight top

When you know the size of your seatpost, you then need to know what kind of top it has. One type of post has a straight top, and the other has an integrated clamp. Knowing which you have makes it easier when it comes time to attach a saddle.

All seatposts have a minimum insertion line. The part of the seatpost under this line *must* be in the frame. Otherwise, you risk your seatpost bending or breaking, not to mention serious injury.

Seatposts are made of steel, aluminum, and carbon fiber. Carbon posts have appeal, but they take more care. Always read the manufacturer's guidelines for your seatpost and use the recommended type of lubricant between the frame and post. Follow the manufacturer's guidelines on seatpost binder torque settings, too.

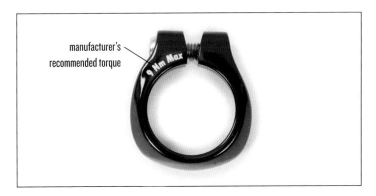

Some manufacturers do not recommend the use of grease between their carbon frames and seatpost. Alternate compounds such as carbon fiber assembly gel are available for such situations.

Some bikes require odd-size seatposts, and it can be hard to find replacements for these. Shims are available to help in these cases. As long as the size difference isn't too great, the shim takes up the required space in the frame. This enables you to use a more common-size seatpost.

When using a shim for your seatpost, it's a good idea to use grease between the seatpost and shim and also between the shim and seat tube. If not greased, these pieces can get stuck together, making it very difficult to adjust them later.

Seatpost Collars

The seatpost collar is the part that keeps your seatpost from sliding down into your frame. That's its only job. You probably don't think about it too much, and rightfully so. But it's an important piece of equipment on your bike.

Seatpost collars come in different sizes, so if you're replacing one, be sure it fits your frame. Measuring the seat tube with a micrometer is ideal. If you don't have access to a micrometer, you can measure the outside diameter of your seat tube with a tape measure instead. That will get you close enough to determine the correct size.

Seatpost collars attach with either a fixing bolt or a quick-release lever.

fixing bolt

quick-release lever

If you have a step-through (ladies') bike and you use a top tube adapter to carry your bike on a car rack, you must keep the quick-release collar tight. That collar is the only thing keeping the back end of your bike on the rack!

Most seatpost collars are printed or stamped with the torque value. This is especially true of bikes with carbon fiber frames. It's very important not to exceed the manufacturer's recommended torque settings. You can measure the torque using a torque wrench. If you don't have this wrench, you can use a standard Allen wrench, but take care—any damage caused by overtightening isn't covered under the manufacturer's warranty.

If you have a steel frame, you probably don't have a seatpost collar. The "collar" is generally built into the frame at the top of the seat tube. To secure the seatpost on this type of bike, you adjust the frame's binder bolt using an Allen wrench.

Suspension Seatposts

To provide more comfort, some bikes come with telescoping
suspension seatposts.

Suspension seatposts have a threaded collar that connects a
sliding shaft to the post, so they soak up some of the bumps in
the road.

Inside the seatpost are a spring and an elastomer that combine to cushion your ride. The spring provides the suspension, and the elastomer keeps the post from bottoming out when you hit a bump. A threaded cap at the bottom of the post enables you to fine-tune the "preload" of the suspension. This is where you can change the feel of the post.

Before you remove your seatpost, it's a good idea to mark it with some electrical tape or a felt pen. Marking the post allows you to put it back in the bike at your original saddle height.

Remove the seatpost from the bike frame, and using an Allen wrench, loosen or tighten the cap to fine-tune the suspension. Don't loosen this cap too much, though. Be sure all the threads are engaged in the bottom of the post.

With this type of seatpost, it's recommended that you periodically check to be sure the collar hasn't become loose. Riding with the collar too loose can result in the threads of the collar—and the seatpost—being ruined. Tightening the collar by hand is all that's required. Be careful to not overtighten.

Determining Your Saddle Height

You cheat yourself if you ride with your saddle too low. When your seat isn't at the correct height, you don't extend your legs enough during the pedal stroke, which can fatigue them prematurely. Riding for many miles with your saddle too low also can cause painful knee issues. If you don't know what your saddle height should be, don't worry. Here you learn two easy ways to determine it.

Measure It

The first way to find your best saddle height is to measure it. The measure you're after is typically referred to as your inseam; it's the height of your pubic bone. To make this measure, you need a ruler or a book, a metric tape measure, and a friend.

Standing in your bare feet and with your feet shoulder width apart, straddle the ruler as you would your bike saddle. Attach the tape measure to the top of the ruler—be sure it's level—and pull up on the ruler as far as you can.

Have your helper measure the distance from the top of the ruler to the floor in centimeters. Take this measurement three times, and write down the largest number of the three. Subtract 10 from this number to get your saddle height in centimeters.

Back at your bike, mark your saddle height, using the number you got from measuring your inseam. Measure from the center of the bottom bracket, up the seat tube, to the top of your saddle.

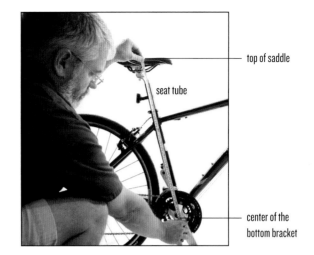

top of saddle

seat tube

center of the bottom bracket

The Straight-Leg Test

The second method is a bit simpler and works especially well if you ride flat pedals.

Get on your bike. Either have a friend hold you up, or put your bike on a stationary trainer. Put your heels on the pedals, and rotate one leg so your foot is at the bottom, dead center of the rotation—picture it at 6 o'clock on a clock face.

Keep your hips level when doing this. If you have to rock your hip to keep your heel on the pedal, lower the saddle and try again. When your leg is straight, your saddle height is correct.

Either one of these saddle adjustments is probably going to preclude you from being able to put your feet on the ground when you're on the saddle. If that makes you uncomfortable, lower the saddle in small increments until you're satisfied. Ultimately, the only "correct" height is the one that doesn't make you uneasy.

straight leg means saddle is at correct height

bent leg means saddle is too low

The Benefits of Bike Shorts

If you have your saddle at the correct height, and the setback and tilt
are where you want them, but you're still not comfortable, you might
want to consider padded cycling shorts. Several types are available to
make your ride more cushioned and comfortable.

The Lycra Short

When people think about cycling shorts, most think of the skin-
tight Lycra variety. These are great for the racer or the avid cyclist
who doesn't want his or her clothing flapping in the wind and
causing drag. The tight fit can also eliminate the chafing that could
occur from your legs going up and down repetitively.

Lycra shorts are constructed with panels. More panels in the short
generally equate to a better fit and increased cost.

The Baggy Short

If you're uncomfortable at the thought of wearing Lycra shorts, you might want to consider a baggy short. As the name implies, the baggy short is a regular-looking short with a padded liner inside. These shorts are often seen on mountain bike trails, but they're also a good option for the casual rider.

Baggy shorts are available with the liners attached or as removable pieces.

The Liner Short

An even better option may be the liner short. This type of short is like a boxer brief with a built-in pad. With a liner short, you can wear your favorite pair of shorts and still have the benefit of a padded cycling short underneath.

Cycling shorts are made specifically for men and for women. Women's shorts tend to feature shorter-length legs. The pads, or *chamois,* are also shaped differently. Like a women's saddle, women's bike shorts are a bit wider in the back, and the front of the pad is shorter as well.

Chapter 9

Pedals

Pedals provide a firm connection between you and your bike. And there have never been so many choices of different types of pedals as there are today. In this chapter, you get to know pedals in their many forms. You read about the different kinds of clipless pedals and how they interface with cycling-specific shoes. You also learn how to install and adjust your cleats. Finally, you look at flat pedals and whether they might be right for you.

Getting to Know Pedals

For all their many forms, there really are only two types of pedals—$1/2$ inch (1.25cm) and $9/16$ inch (1.5cm). The difference is the size of the spindle where it threads into the crank arm.

How can you tell which is which? Look to the crank.

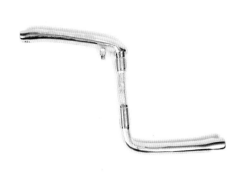

one-piece crank

three-piece crank

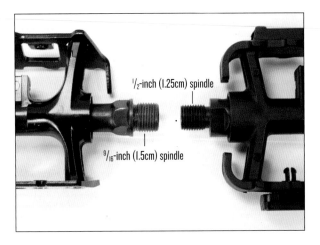

$1/2$-inch (1.25cm) spindle

$9/16$-inch (1.5cm) spindle

If you have a bike with a one-piece crank, the pedals are $1/2$ inch (1.25cm). If your bike has a three-piece crank, your pedals are $9/16$ inch (1.5cm). Both spindle sizes use 20 threads per inch (tpi).

Once you've determined the size of your pedal, the only other thing you need to know is which pedal is the left pedal and which is the right. Each pedal should be marked with L or R. The right pedal goes on the drive side of the bike.

On occasion, you might find pedals that either aren't marked or the marking is so faint you can't read it. What then? There's an easy way you can tell left from right if the pedal isn't marked: if the thread falls to the right, it's the left pedal. If the thread falls to the left, it's the right pedal.

thread falls to the left, so this is the right pedal

The left pedal always has a reverse thread. That means turning the spindle to the left tightens the pedal, and turning the spindle to the right loosens it.

The Simplicity of Flat Pedals

There's a freedom and joy that comes from being able to just jump on your bike and ride—no special clothing, no special shoes, no special equipment (except your helmet, of course). It's liberating, and it's fun.

Flat pedals—the type of pedals you probably learned to ride your bike—are a good, basic choice. They're nice for new riders and those who aren't entirely comfortable being clipped in to a pedal all the time.

Riding with flat pedals means you can get off your bike and walk into a shop, stop and take a photograph, or ride to dinner without clomping into the restaurant in your clip-in bike shoes. No need to worry about getting unclipped at stop signs. No struggle to get into your pedals when the light turns green. The grippers on the pedals keep your feet in place, and you just spin along. It's all about enjoying the ride.

Riding with a flat pedal allows you to move your foot around as you ride. You can slide your foot back so the ball of your foot is at or behind the spindle when you're riding on flat ground. Or you can slide your foot forward so your arch is over the spindle during a seated climb. That's not possible when you're clipped in to your pedals.

When you ride wearing regular shoes and using standard flat pedals, you can experience some unwanted shoe flex that can lead to foot and leg fatigue on longer rides. Luckily, some fantastic flat pedals are available that are significantly larger to avoid this problem.

Odyssey Twisted PC and MKS Lambda pedals are two of my favorites. Both of these pedals are significantly larger than a standard flat pedal. The increased size provides the stiffness you need and a great grip.

If you're uncomfortable with the thought of being "locked" to the pedal, or you've never been able to find a pair a cycling shoes that fit your feet, give a pair of flat pedals a try.

Odyssey Twisted PC pedal

MKS Lambda pedal

A Look at Clipless Pedals

Sometime in the 1980s, a manufacturer named Look put its ski-binding technology into bicycle pedals. These pedals fixed your foot to the pedal via a cleat on your shoe but contained no straps or clips—hence *clipless* pedals.

After riding your new bike for a while, you might start thinking about getting clipless pedals. Maybe all your friends have them and recommend you might like them, too. But are they for you?

A clipless pedal, combined with a compatible shoe that contains a cleat that locks into the pedal, connects you to your bike. That connection can be a little unnerving at first, especially because you can't just step off your pedal and put your foot on the ground to steady yourself. But eventually you get used it to it—particularly when you feel that new level of control over your machine you might not have felt when you're riding "free."

Compared to a standard flat pedal and athletic shoe, the clipless pedal and shoe combination provides a much stiffer platform. This means more of your power goes straight to the pedal. It can also lessen foot fatigue on long rides.

Being connected to the pedal enables you to pull up on the pedal as well as push down. This can be helpful when you're climbing or when you're mountain biking and riding up and over obstacles is common.

When you first get your clipless pedals, practice riding with them in a quiet cul-de-sac or a large, empty parking lot. This gives you a chance to get used to getting in and out of your pedals before you hit the road or trail.

On your first few clipless rides, you'll be very aware that you are "locked" to the bike. In a short time, however, you become accustomed to this feeling. Don't be surprised if you roll up to a stop sign, forget that you're clipped in, and fall over. It's normal, and it's happened to nearly everyone who tries clipless pedals.

Some riders just aren't comfortable with the idea of being locked to the pedal, and that's okay. Riding a bike should be about having fun, not conforming to what anyone else thinks.

If you're thinking about racing, or even riding with racers, the small size of most clipless pedals makes pedaling through corners easier.

Types of Clipless Pedals

You've decided to make the switch to clipless pedals, but which pedal do you choose? Pedals are generally grouped into one of two categories, road bike pedals or mountain bike pedals.

Road Bike Pedals

Road bike pedals are designed to keep weight to a minimum. They're usually quite thin, lessening the likelihood of you hitting the pedal on the ground if you pedal through a turn.

Because you clip in at the back of the pedal, the entry on a road bike pedal is a bit different. When your foot is not in the pedal, the weight of the retention mechanism naturally falls to the bottom. Clipping in requires you to catch the front of the pedal with the front of your cleat and then step down to engage the cleat in the retention mechanism.

front of pedal

retention mechanism

Mountain Bike Pedals

Mountain bike pedals are double-sided, meaning you can clip into the pedal on either side. All these pedals use a cleat that attaches to the shoe with two bolts.

The construction of mountain bike pedals is usually open so you can better deal with the dirt and mud you encounter during off-road riding. These pedals also work very well for recreational riders and tourists.

Double-Sided Pedals

If you're not sure you want to be clipped in all the time, some very nice double-sided pedals are available. These pedals feature a clipless pedal on one side and a flat pedal on the other.

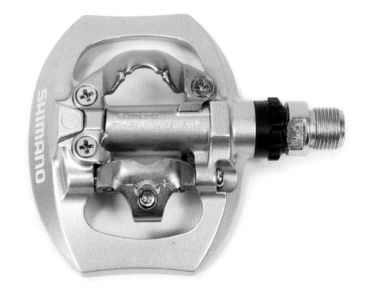

> Although entry can vary among pedals, getting out is the same for all: to remove your foot from the pedal, simply turn your heel out.

Cycling-Specific Shoes

Your feet represent two of the five contact points between your body and your bike. (Your hands and your rear end are the other three.) If you're going to wear cycling shoes, it's very important to find a pair that fits properly. A good deal on any old pair of cycling shoes ceases to be a good deal when your feet are hurting you 10 minutes into an all-day ride.

Cycling shoes should be snug but not tight. When you're standing, you should have no more than a thumb's width of space between your longest toe and the front of the shoe.

A *last* is the form a manufacturer uses to make a pair of shoes. Each manufacturer uses a slightly different last. Not only that, but lasts can be different among models from the same manufacturer. So no two pairs of shoes fit exactly the same. If one pair doesn't work for you, try another one.

Road Shoes

Road shoes are lightweight and very stiff. They typically have nylon or carbon soles, and the closures are generally Velcro or a combination of Velcro and buckles. The cleat mounts to the bottom of the sole and is not meant for walking.

Mountain Shoes

Mountain bike shoes share many of the characteristics of road shoes. The difference is mainly in the sole. Mountain shoes have lugged rubber soles and a recessed spot for the cleat.

Mountain shoes work well for the rider who rides on and off road and wants a shoe that can be walked in.

Walkable Road Shoes

The walkable road shoe is a modern-day version of the touring shoe, the original walkable road shoe. They feature a road shoe upper with a rubber sole that accepts a recessed cleat. They're generally lighter than mountain shoes due to the lack lugs on the sole.

For the recreational rider who still wants the benefits of a cycling shoe, this might be the ideal choice.

Using a Pedal Wrench

If you've ever tried to remove your pedals without a pedal wrench, you might have found it a bit challenging. Most regular open-ended wrenches aren't thin enough and also don't provide the leverage required to remove a pedal. The pedal wrench solves both problems.

When replacing a pedal, always start tightening them by hand. The quickest way to cross-thread your pedals is to immediately put a wrench on them. Ideally, you should be able to thread pedals on by hand, only using the wrench for the final tightening.

To remove your right (drive-side) pedal, put your wrench on the pedal so the handle points toward the back of the bike. Holding the left crank arm in your right hand, push the pedal wrench down with your left hand. Take care when you do this. The pedal can "let go" quite quickly, and you don't want to run your hand into the chainring.

Remember, the left pedal has a reverse thread, so you remove the left pedal much the same way you do the right. With the drive side crank arm facing the front of the bike, put the wrench on the left pedal with the handle pointing toward the front of the bike. Hold the right crank arm with your left hand, and pull the wrench up with your right hand.

Some pedals don't have flats on the spindle for a wrench to fit onto. Instead, these pedals have Allen wrench holes, so you need a different wrench. The theory behind these pedals was by taking away the flat, people would be less inclined to overtighten their pedals. These pedals can be a bit more of a challenge to remove because you have less room to operate "inside" the bike. You still turn both pedals counterclockwise to remove them.

Adjusting Pedal Tension

Most clipless pedals have the option to increase or decrease the tension required to get into or out of the pedal. This can be especially helpful when you first start clipping in.

To adjust the tension on a mountain bike pedal, locate the small hex bolts on both sides of the pedal. These bolts have a right-hand thread, so turning them clockwise tightens and turning them counterclockwise loosen them. The bolts have stops so you know how many "clicks" you're turning them. When in doubt, most pedals have directional arrows showing which way to turn for more or less tension.

When adjusting the tension on this type of pedal, it's important that all sides be the same. Because the pedal is double-sided, you have separate tension adjustment for each side. Therefore, it's a good idea to turn all the adjusting bolts fully to one side and then turn each bolt the same number of clicks back.

Some entry-level road pedals come with a relatively low preset tension. You can't adjust these pedals.

Adjusting the tension on a road pedal is the same, but there's only one bolt per pedal.

Installing and Adjusting Cleats

Every pair of clipless pedals comes with a set of cleats. The cleats are what enable your shoe to attach to your pedal, and they are specific to each type of pedal.

1 You're going to need a screwdriver or Allen wrench (it will vary from pedal to pedal) and some grease (preferably waterproof). If you're using a mountain bike or walkable road shoe, you might have some extra prep to do. For example, some shoes have a cover over the cleat area you need to remove before you can begin installation.

2 Insert a flat screwdriver under the cover to pry it off. After you have it started with the screwdriver, you should be able to pull off the plate the rest of the way by hand.

3 The cleat area on some other shoes is open, but the cleat nut that receives the bolts might not be not installed. To install it, remove the shoe's insole, and insert the cleat nut inside the shoe. There's no front or back, but there is an obvious spot where it fits in the shoe.

When installing cleats, it's helpful to hold the cleat nut in place until you get the first bolt started. Put one hand inside the shoe, and hold the plate in place until the first bolt is in place. After that, the plate shouldn't move.

4 After the cleat nut is installed, reinsert the insole.

5 Put a small amount of grease on the bolts.

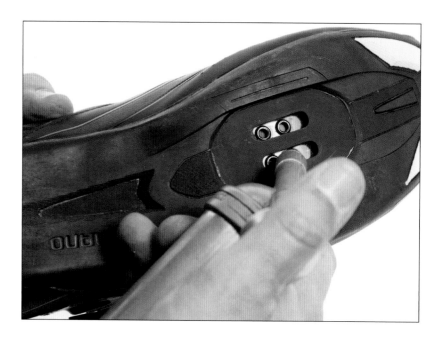

6 Position your cleat so the ball of your big toe will be at or slightly in front of the pedal spindle, and tighten the hex bolts.

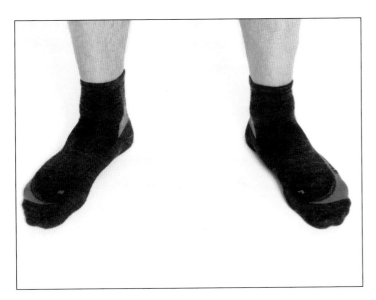

Most people don't walk with their feet pointed exactly straight ahead, and because you want your cleats to mimic the natural position of your feet, you need to account for this when installing and adjusting your cleats.

To do this, have someone watch you walk in your bare feet and note the way your feet naturally land. Note each foot might be different. If you naturally walk with your toes pointed out, the cleats on that foot should be slightly rotated to match.

If you experience knee pain after installing your cleats, consider consulting a bike-fitting professional for a proper cleat adjustment.

If you're unsure about where the ball of your foot is, there's an easy way to find it. Standing with your cycling shoes on, locate the knuckle of your big toe. Place a piece of tape on that spot, and use it as a reference for the front and back cleat placement.

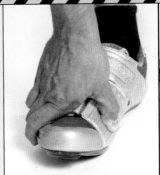

Recognizing Cleat Wear

The cleat is the connection between your shoe and your pedal. It's small and doesn't require a lot of maintenance, so it's easy to neglect.

Cleats wear naturally as you get into and out of your clipless pedals. And if you walk in your shoes, the cleat wears much faster.

At some point, it will be visually obvious the cleat is worn. I've seen cleats so worn, the tops of the fixing bolts were worn down, too. Worn cleats present a few problems.

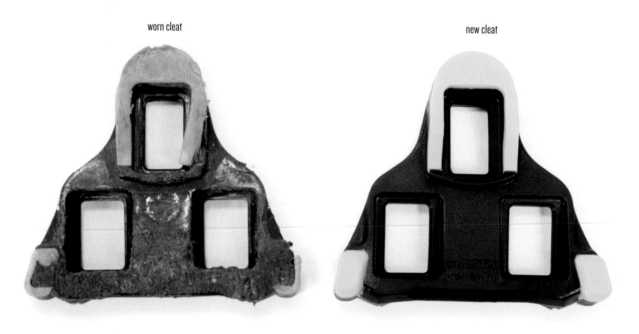

worn cleat   new cleat

Most new cleats are set up for a limited amount of "float." This means that when you're secured into your pedal, your foot isn't locked into a completely fixed position and can move slightly. As the cleat, wears this float can increase and may lead to knee problems.

With an excessively worn cleat, the points of engagement between the pedal and cleat are degraded. This can result in your foot coming out of the pedal prematurely, possibly causing a crash.

Cleat wear might not be entirely visible. If you feel excessive play in your pedals, your cleats probably need to be replaced.

If you must walk in your bike shoes, use cleat covers. These small plastic covers protect your cleats from the damage walking causes.

When it's time to replace your cleats, use a felt pen to trace on your shoe where the old cleat was. That way, you're sure to get the new cleat back in the same position.

Chapter 10
Steering Systems

The front end of your bike not only houses the parts that enable you to steer your bike, it's also the main point of control for you as you're riding, via your hands on the handlebars. And because it's a place where your body contacts the bike, it's also an area where adjustments can have a great impact on your comfort. In this chapter, you get a look at the different types of steering systems. You also learn how to adjust a headset, adjust the height of your handlebars, install new bar tape, and more.

Quill Versus Threadless Stems

A lot happens at the front of your bike. You steer from here as well as shift and brake from your handlebars. Your handlebars are obviously important, but so is the piece that connects your handlebars to your bike's frame: the stem. Stems come in two types: quill and threadless.

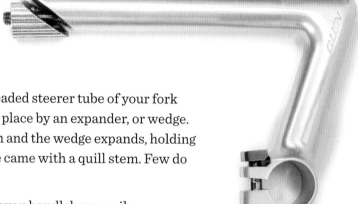

Quill Stems

The kind of stem that slides into the threaded steerer tube of your fork is called a *quill stem*. This stem is held in place by an expander, or wedge. You tighten the bolt at the top of the stem and the wedge expands, holding the stem in place. At one time, every bike came with a quill stem. Few do now.

A quill stem enables you to raise or lower you handlebars easily.

The downside of a quill stem is that few had removable faceplates. That meant more work every time you needed to change handlebars. A new handlebar meant removing the tape on at least one side of the bar and one brake lever so you could slide the bar through the clamp area of the stem. When the new bar was installed, you'd have to reinstall the lever and retape the bar.

Threadless Stems

These days, bikes come with *threadless stems*. These stems clamp directly onto the fork's steerer tube. Threadless stems are lighter than the quill type, and the removable faceplates enable you to remove the handlebars without taking off the tape or brake levers.

The downside of a threadless stem is that the height of the handlebar is limited by the length of the steerer tube. On most bikes, this length is predetermined. Without taking extra measures, like adding a steerer tube extender, the bars are as high as they're ever going to be.

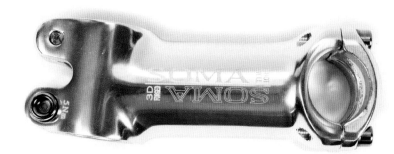

Adapters

If you have a threaded steerer but you'd rather use a threadless stem, adapters are available. They're basically the quill without the stem. To install, slide the adapter into your fork and tighten as you would a normal quill stem. Then you can clamp a threadless stem onto the adapter.

An adapter is also available if you want to use your quill stem on a threadless steerer. This adapter mimics the threadless headset, keeping the steerer tube open for your quill stem.

Handlebar Types and Sizes

It's easy to overlook the importance of your handlebars, but they are responsible for two of the five contact points on your bike (along with your two feet and your backside), and your hands spend a lot of time in contact with them. If you're having issues with hand comfort, a handlebar switch could be the solution.

Road Bike Handlebars

A road bike handlebar is made up of the *tops, ramps, hooks,* and *drops.*

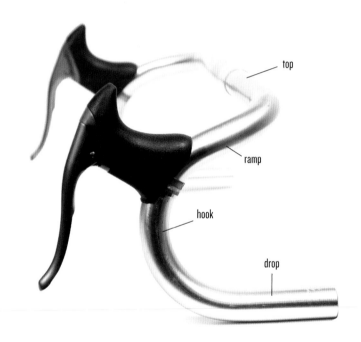

Bars are available in a variety of widths, and varying widths can impact your comfort on the bike. Historically, bars the width of your shoulder blades were the norm, but you might prefer one wider or narrower.

The majority of road bars are available in two clamp sizes, 26.0 millimeters and 31.8 millimeters.

26.0-millimeter bar

31.8-millimeter bar

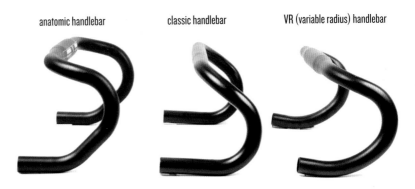

Bars also are available in different shapes, and each has a unique feel. As the shape and bend changes, so does the distance from the ramps of the bar to the drops—a distance also called the drop.

The ramp, the area on top of the bar directly behind the brake lever, is where your hands probably spend most of the time they're in contact with the handlebars. One of the big improvements in handlebars in recent years has been the flattening out of the ramp area. This provides a much larger—and more comfortable—space for your hands.

Mountain Bike Handlebars

Mountain bike handlebars, once mostly flat, now come in a variety of sweeps, bends, and angles—and they're appropriate for more than just mountain bikes. The same riser-type bars you find on current mountain bikes are also used on comfort and hybrid bikes. The clamp size for a mountain bike handlebar is generally either 25.4 millimeters or 31.8 millimeters.

If your mountain bike is used for more than just riding off road, the single hand position of a flat or riser bar might be too limiting. Some bars put your hands in a more natural position, and some provide multiple hand positions. As long as the bar and stem are the same size, there's no one right or wrong bar. Don't be afraid to experiment.

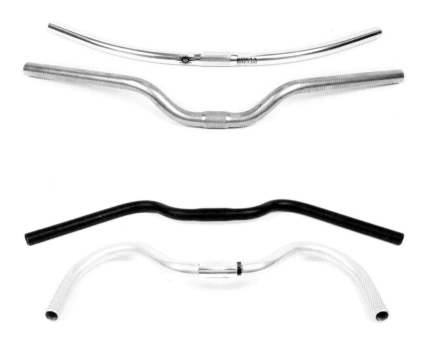

Headset Types

Your bike's headset is made of a number of parts that work together to enable you to turn and balance your bicycle. Every headset includes a *crown race* that presses onto your fork, a set of *bearings* for the top and bottom of the headset, and an *upper and lower cup* for the bearings to rest in. The bearings can be either loose or sealed, and the cups can either press into the frame or be part of the frame itself. In the case of a threadless headset, you also have a top cap and bolt that control the headset adjustment.

At first glance, it might seem like headsets come in many different types and sizes. But for the most part, they come in two common types: threaded and threadless.

The Threaded Headset

The threaded headset was the standard on bikes for decades. Although once there were many different 1-inch (25.4mm) headsets, just two are common now: the ISO (International Standard Organization) and JIS (Japanese Industrial Standard) headsets.

These two headsets are nearly identical except for one small detail: the ISO headset uses a crown race that's 26.4 millimeters, and the JIS uses one that's 27.0 millimeters. It doesn't seem like a big difference, but it's enough that they're not interchangeable.

The 1^1/$_8$-inch (28.6mm) headset is most common these days. The 1-inch (25.4mm) headset is found mostly on older bikes.

1-inch (25.4mm) headset

1^1/$_8$-inch (28.6mm) headset

The Threadless Headset

Threadless headsets also can come in 1-inch (25.4mm) and $1^1/_8$-inch (28.6mm) sizes. The $1^1/_8$-inch (28.6mm) headset is the most common size on current bikes, but you still see some bikes—triathlon bikes, for example—that use the 1-inch (25.4mm) size.

Threadless headsets are different because they don't thread onto the steerer tube, but instead used a star nut that's pressed into the fork for adjustment.

For a number of years, the trend has been moving away from headsets with external cups (cups that are pressed into the frame's headtube). Whether for looks or weight, these headsets have bearings that sit inside the headtube. They can be broken down into two types, integrated headsets and internal headsets.

There is a $1^1/_4$-inch (31.8mm) "oversized" threadless headset, but it's used mainly on tandem bicycles.

The Integrated Headset

An integrated headset features a set of bearings that sit inside a cup that's part of the headtube. This type of headset contains very few parts, but any damage that occurs to the headset could damage the frame as well.

The Internal Headset

The bearings of an internal headset still reside within the headtube, but they do have cups pressed into the headtube. Because of this, the headset cups can be removed and replaced if necessary.

Adjusting Threaded Headsets

The headset is the part of the bike that allows for turning and balancing. A threaded headset is made up of a *crown race* that's pressed onto the crown of the fork, a *lower race* that's pressed into the bottom of the head tube, an *upper threaded race, spacers,* and a *lock nut.*

A headset that's too loose can compromise turning and balancing. A headset that's too tight can lead to unresponsive steering and cause the headset to prematurely wear.

To adjust a threaded headset, you need one—and preferably two—headset wrenches. Both the upper race and the lock nut have a right-hand thread, so to tighten them, turn them clockwise.

The upper race is where you make any adjustments, but first you need to loosen the lock nut. (You don't have to remove the stem to adjust your headset.)

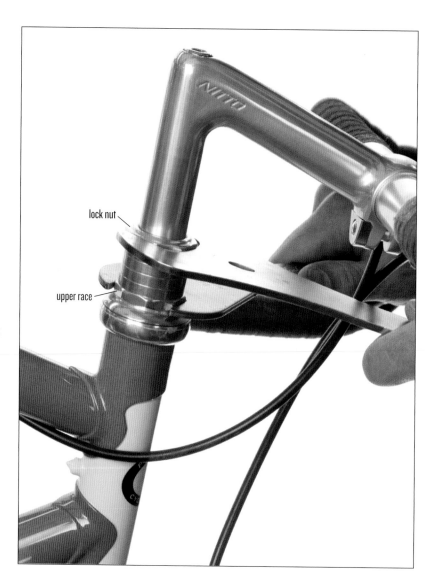

lock nut

upper race

If the headset is loose, tighten the upper race slightly. Holding the upper race in place, tighten the lock nut a bit and then check the adjustment. You should be able to turn the handlebars from side to side freely. If the wheel sticks or feels rough at any point, the headset might be too tight.

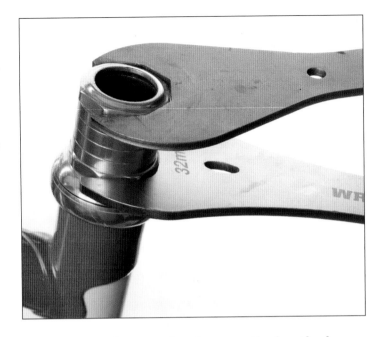

As a second way to check the adjustment, set your bike on the ground and squeeze the front brake tightly. Rock the front wheel forward and back. If you feel movement, or if you hear a popping sound, the headset is too loose. Repeat the adjustment process until the adjustment is correct.

Historically, threaded steerer tubes had a groove cut into them, and the headset came with a keyed washer. Used together, these two pieces would keep the upper race from moving when you tightened the lock nut. The result—in theory anyway—was that you could adjust the headset with only one wrench. In practice, however, these keyed washers seldom stay in place. You're better off using two wrenches.

key in groove

keyed washer

threaded steerer

groove

Adjusting Threadless Headsets

What the threadless headset lacks in vertical adjustability, it makes up for in ease of adjustment. How do you know if your headset needs to be adjusted? The bars should move freely when you turn them side to side. If they bind at any point, the headset is probably too tight. If you feel play in the headset when you apply the front brake, the headset is too loose.

To adjust a threadless headset, you need one or possibly two sizes of Allen wrenches.

pinch bolts

1 The threadless headset uses compression to keep everything together. So before you can change the adjustment of the headset, you must loosen the pinch bolts on the stem.

With this system, the top cap and stem pinch bolts can be the only thing holding the fork in the frame. If you're using a work stand, it's a good idea to secure the front wheel with a bungee cord or toe strap before you loosen the headset.

And if your bike has cantilever brakes, you'll have to loosen the cable stop pinch bolt (if it has one) before you can adjust the headset.

2 Using your Allen wrench, tighten or loosen the bolt in the top cap just enough to take the play out of the headset.

top cap bolt

pinch bolts

3 Check your adjustment with the bike on the ground. Squeeze the front brake and rock the bike forward. If you feel play in the headset, it needs to be readjusted. After you've made the adjustment and checked that it's correct, tighten the pinch bolts on the stem.

What if you've adjusted your headset but it still has play? Check your spacers. Your stem should clear the steerer tube by approximately $\frac{1}{8}$ inch (3.25mm). If the stem is flush with the steerer tube, the headset won't tighten. Add the necessary spacer or spacers, and readjust.

Installing Aero Bars

You might have seen some cyclists riding with unique-looking handlebars that give the rider an elbow rest and then extend out over the front wheel and have a forward-pointing grip the rider can hold onto. These are called aero bars. Aero bar extensions give long-distance cyclists another riding position and provide welcome relief for riders who spend many miles on open, windy roads.

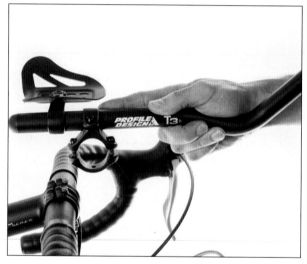

Although originally designed for triathlon bikes, clip-on aero bars have become very popular with a wide range of cyclists. The bars come in more shapes and are much more adjustable than their predecessors.

Most aero bar extensions are built for 31.8-millimeter handlebars, but they should come with shims for the smaller 26.0-millimeter handlebars as well.

Clamping aero bars to carbon handlebars can potentially crush the bars. Always check compatibility before you mount any aero extension on your carbon bars.

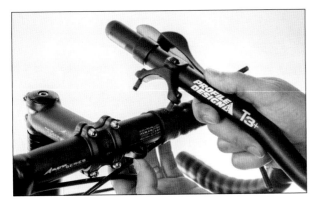

1 To install, first disassemble the bracket, and position the extensions on your handlebar on the bulge area just adjacent to the stem—basically the center of the bar. You only have a *very* small space in which you can adjust the bars.

2 When you have the aero bars where you want them, align the holes in the bottom part of the bracket with the bolts in the upper part.

3 Using an Allen wrench, tighten the bolts to secure, following any torque settings the manufacturer recommends.

4 Some bars come with the armrests already installed. If yours aren't, use the supplied tools to affix the armrests to the extensions, and install the armrest pads.

Multiple holes are available to use when placing your armrests. If they're preinstalled, they're likely to fit in the center position. If you have very broad or very narrow shoulders, don't be afraid to move the arm rests out or in as necessary until you find a comfortable position for you.

The riding position aero bar extensions allow can potentially change the way your bike handles. As with anything new, start slowly to allow yourself time to get accustomed to this new position.

Raising Your Handlebars

If you could make one change to your bike, what would it be? If you said, "Raise my handlebars," you aren't alone. This is often the top complaint people have about their bikes. Fortunately, it's an easy fix— and one that can make a big difference in your comfort as you ride.

Before you get started, to hold the front wheel and handlebars steady, use something like a bungee cord or a toe strap to secure the wheel to the frame.

Raising Threadless Stems

With a threadless stem, you have two options to raise your bars. The first is to opt for a stem with more angle. This works well if you only need to raise the bars slightly.

The second, and easiest, way to raise your handlebars with a threadless stem is by using a steerer tube extender. You install this just as you would a stem, and when the extender is in place, your stem clamps to it. You can raise your bars 2 or 3 inches (5 to 7.5cm) with an extender, but you also might need to replace some cables.

> Remember, when you replace your stem with one that has more rise, you are also bringing the bar back toward you. If you want to keep your reach the same, the stem needs to be higher *and* longer.

1 Start by removing the top cap of your headset using an Allen wrench.

2 Loosen the pinch bolts on your stem and remove the stem from the steerer tube.

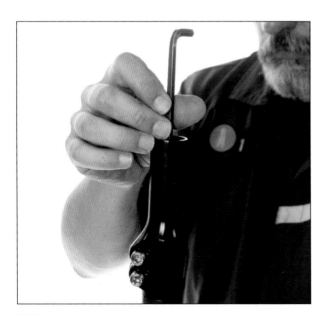

3 Install the steerer tube extender, and use an Allen wrench to tighten the center bolt to the headset.

4 Install your stem on the extender.

5 Straighten the extender, and tighten the pinch bolts.

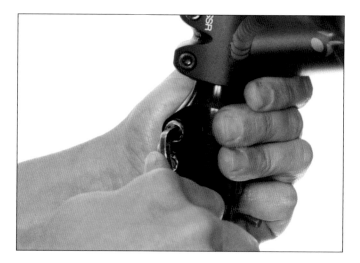

6 Center your handlebars, and tighten the pinch bolts on the stem.

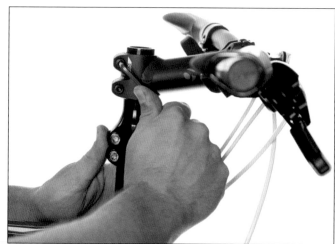

7 Reinstall the top cap to finish the job.

Raising Quill Stems

If you've got a quill stem, you have a couple options. Here's the first:

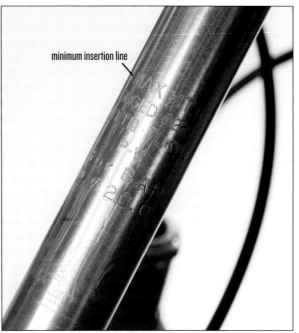

minimum insertion line

1 Using an Allen wrench, loosen the bolt on top of the stem. The stem should now slide up and down. If it doesn't, you might need to loosen the bolt a little more and give the stem a gentle tap with a hammer.

2 When the stem is loose, pull it out until you see the minimum insertion line. Remember, this line represents how much of the stem needs to be in the steerer tube in order to be safe. If you're not at the line, raise your stem.

If you're already at the limit for your stem, or if the amount the stem could be raised wasn't enough, you could use an extender. An extender basically lengthens your stem's quill. To use an extender, insert it into the fork, paying attention to the minimum insertion line, and tighten the bolt as you would the bolt on your stem. Then insert the stem into the extender, and repeat the tightening process with your stem as you did with the extender.

Stems with longer quills are also available. This is a more expensive option, but often it's more the attractive one. Whichever option you choose, you probably need to replace some or all of the cables on your bike to compensate for the height difference.

Removing and Rewrapping Handlebar Tape

Installing new handlebar tape is the easiest, least-expensive way to give your bike a fresh, clean look. Best of all, it's not as hard as you might think.

Handlebar tape comes in a wide variety of colors. After you've chosen one, it's time to strip off that old, dirty tape.

1 Fold back the hoods on your brake levers to expose the ends of the tape. Begin unwrapping. Note how the old tape comes off, and it could make reversing the process easier.

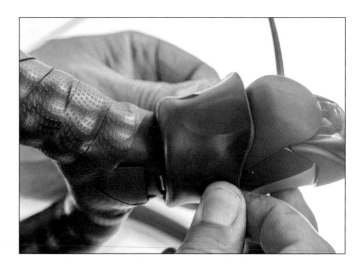

2 Most packages of tape come with two precut sections about 2 inches (5cm) long. Place these over the clamp of your brake lever.

There are two ways to start the taping process. Some people leave a bit of tape hanging over the end of the bar and use the bar end plug to secure the tape. Others overlap the tape at the beginning, letting friction hold the tape in place. Either way works. Experiment and see which way you like best.

3 Starting at the bottom of your handlebar, begin to work the tape up and around your handlebars. The tape needs to be taut, but don't pull too tight or it will tear.

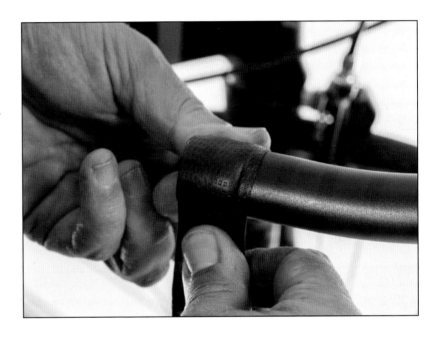

4 As you wrap, overlap the tape about $1/2$ inch (2.5cm) each pass.

5 Wrap the tape up and over the brake lever. Be sure you don't leave any gaps in the tape. You don't want the bar showing through.

6 When you get to the middle of the bar, cut the tape at an angle. This leaves a consistent thickness in the tape.

7 Most packages also include a finishing tape you can use to hold the end of the bar tape in place. This tape works, but plain black electrical tape holds much better.

8 Insert the bar plug.

9 Pull the brake lever hood back in place and you're done.

If you later notice you missed a spot halfway through, it's not a problem. Most tapes can be unwrapped and wrapped again. Keep trying until you get it just right.

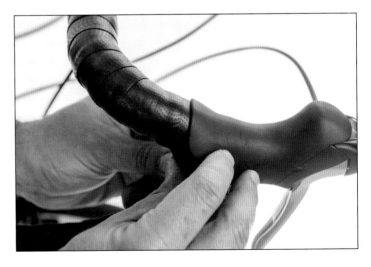

Removing and Installing Mountain Bike Grips

If you have a mountain bike, the grips on your handle bars provide some padding, cut down on vibration, and maybe even add a little color to your bike. Most are made out of rubber, so they do wear out.

When you decide to replace your grips, the hardest part of the task is getting off the old grips.

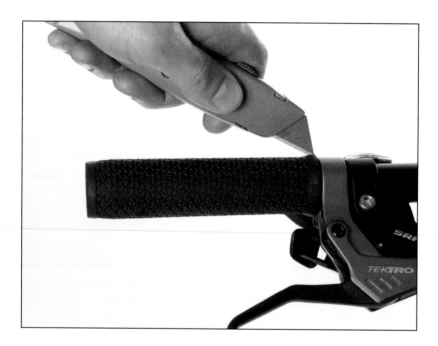

If you're not planning on saving the grips, you can carefully cut them off using a utility knife. If you do want to save them, try spraying some window cleaner under the edge of the grip. That should make them slippery enough to slide off. If necessary, you also can use a small screwdriver to get under the grip. If your bike has carbon bars, be careful not to scratch them.

  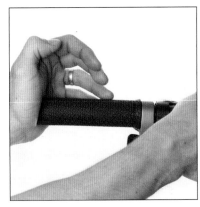

Before you install your new grips, be sure the handlebar is clean and dry. You want the grips to slide on easily, but you want them to stay put once they're on. Spray a little hair spray inside the grip. It makes the grips easier to put on, and it dries tacky, keeping the grips in place.

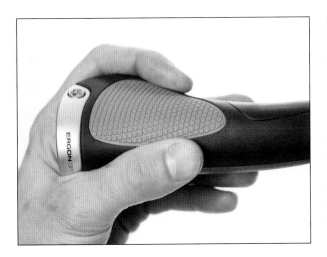 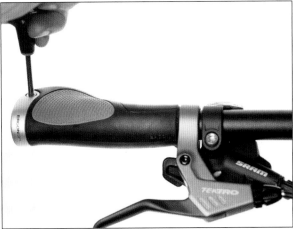

Some grips have collars that lock on the handlebar. These are nice because they go on the bar very easily. Use an Allen wrench to tighten the collars. As always, be careful not to overtighten the bolts.

Everyone has his or her own idea about what's comfortable. Some like a round grip, while others prefer an ergonomic grip like the one shown here. These ergonomic grips have become more popular over the last few years because they give you a bigger platform upon which to rest your hands. If you experience hand discomfort when riding, you might give them a try.

STEERING SYSTEMS

Steering System Safety

It's natural to want to change your riding position from time to time. Maybe your bike isn't as comfortable as it once was. Or maybe it's been a while since you rode a bike or your bike isn't quite the right size anymore. Before you make any changes to your bike's steering system, it's important to understand its limitations.

One of the benefits of an older-style quill stem is the capability to raise the stem and handlebars. Each stem is stamped with a minimum insertion line. This represents the amount of stem that must be inside the steerer tube to be safe. Riding with the stem above this line could cause a serious crash if the stem fails while you're riding.

You should periodically check the bolt that clamps the handlebar into the stem. Be sure it's tight and ensure no cracks have formed in the stem or handlebar.

If you have a threadless system, your bike comes with the exact number of spacers required to make the system work. The spacers can be moved around but not subtracted from or added to. The stem needs to clear the steerer tube by approximately $1/8$ inches (3.2mm). This provides the compression required to keep the headset tight.

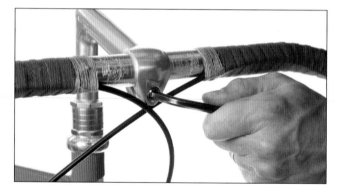

The stem's upper pinch bolt must not extend above the top of the steerer tube. This could result in the stem being held in place by only one bolt, and this obviously is not safe.

If you lower your stem, you must relocate the spacers above the stem. Failure to do this could result in the top cap pushing only against the steerer tube, and the headset won't tighten.

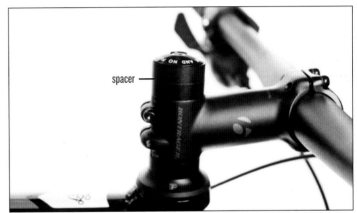

Check the fixing bolts on your stem's faceplate periodically. All bolts should be tightened uniformly and to the manufacturer's torque values.

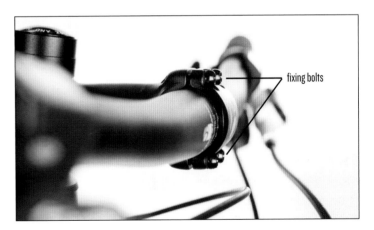

If your fork has a carbon steerer, the manufacturer might require a spacer of at least 5mm above the stem. Always consult the manufacturer's guidelines before making any changes.

The Benefits of Gloves

It might seem odd to talk about gloves in this chapter, but when most riders think about cycling gloves, they think of them as an accessory to increase comfort. This is partially correct, but it's not the only reason to wear cycling gloves.

Pro cyclists wear gloves so that, in the case of a fall, their hands are protected. Gloves also give them the ability to wipe their tires after they ride through debris. These gloves rarely, if ever, have much padding.

In addition to protection, you can wear gloves for comfort and to decrease any vibration you feel through the handlebar. Padded gloves can decrease hand numbness caused by pressure on the ulnar nerve, a nerve that runs along the outside of the palm, up the arm, and to the neck. On hot days, gloves can keep your sweaty hands from slipping on the handlebar.

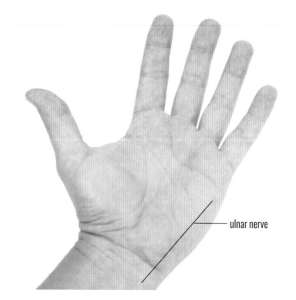

ulnar nerve

Most often, fingerless, recreational cyclist gloves can be found with foam or gel padding built in to the palm of the glove to help cushion your ulnar nerve.

Even in the summer months, it's not uncommon to wear full-fingered gloves while mountain biking. These gloves provide an extra measure of grip and protection over the fingerless variety.

A glove that fits properly can be a challenge to remove. Try pulling them off so they end up inside out. They'll come off faster and easier.

Chapter 11

Frames

Your bike's frame is more than just the thing you bolt various parts to—it's the structural centerpiece of your bike. In this chapter, you learn about the different frame materials currently used for bike frames and how they can affect the way your bike rides. You also discover how to keep your bike looking new by keeping it clean and find out what to do if your frame is damaged.

Types of Frames

The number of materials used to make bicycle frames seems to grow every year. Wood, bamboo, and even cardboard—yes, cardboard—have all been used to make frames.

Someday, some of these materials might become mainstream frame materials, but until then, let's look at the materials that are widely available in today's bikes.

Carbon Fiber

Carbon fiber has become so prevalent as a bike frame material, it seems like it's been around forever. In reality, carbon fiber has only been favored for higher-end bikes for the last decade.

Carbon starts as sheets of the material. Along with resin, the sheets are pressed into molds and cured. The resulting frames are very light, and because the carbon sheets are woven in one direction, they can be layered inside the mold in different directions, enabling the manufacturer to "tune" the ride.

Carbon has the reputation of absorbing road shock. Because of the nature of the material, it could be that it merely handles the vibration in a different way. The end result for you, however, is typically less perceived road shock.

Carbon fiber is very strong and quite durable. Carbon fiber frames, however, do not hold up as well to impacts as metal frames.

What about titanium? That's a good question. Some people thought titanium would be *the* material for bikes. It has the weight of aluminum but many of the ride qualities of steel. But the fact that the material is harder to work with, coupled with the influx of carbon fiber, has kept titanium from becoming a widely used material in bike frames.

Aluminum

The first aluminum bikes were roughly a third the weight of their steel counterparts. At one point, this made aluminum the preferred lightweight alternative for bike frames. But as prices on carbon fiber frames drop, the use of aluminum is dropping as well. But it's comparatively low cost still makes it an ideal material for a bicycle frame.

In the early days of aluminum bike frames, the bikes were not only lightweight but also stiff. That stiffness, especially early on, earned aluminum bikes a reputation of being unforgiving. As manufacturing processes have improved, so has the ride of aluminum frames.

Aluminum is the most used material in the bicycle world right now. Frames, rims, cranks, and most components are made of some sort of aluminum.

Steel

Steel frames offer a resilient, almost springy ride. Steel is strong, and it doesn't tend to fail—much less fail catastrophically. But steel has fallen out of favor as other, lighter materials have become available for bike frames.

Durability, strength, and the capability to mount accessories like racks and fenders have kept steel the choice material for touring bikes.

A Look at Derailleur Hangers

The spot where your rear derailleur connects to your frame is called the *derailleur hanger*. The hanger and its alignment have as much to do with shifting performance as the derailleur itself. Damaging a derailleur hanger most often happens when a rear derailleur overshifts into the rear wheel.

If you have an older bike, the hanger is actually part of the rear dropout. At one time, it wasn't uncommon for hangers on steel bikes to become bent. For an experienced mechanic, it was a relatively easy fix to bend them back using an alignment tool. In extreme cases, you could give your bike to a frame builder, and he'd cut out the old dropout and install a new one in its place.

As materials have changed, repairing damaged hangers has become more difficult—and potentially much more expensive. Because of this, manufacturers have started using replaceable derailleur hangers.

It's much less expensive to replace a derailleur hanger than it is to have an entire frame repaired—or worse yet, replaced. Replacing a hanger is something almost any rider can do. It doesn't require any special tools or extensive technical knowledge.

Not all bikes use the same hanger, so you need to know which hanger your bike uses. At first, if you had bike brand *X,* you would have to visit a dealer who sold that brand of bike to purchase a replacement hanger. As these replacement parts have become more common, third parties have started making them, much to the convenience of consumers.

The thing to realize about replaceable hangers is that they're designed to break. If you crash, it's better for the hanger to break and not the frame. If your derailleur hanger breaks, you might have to replace the derailleur, the hanger, and the rear wheel, but the frame remains intact.

You might be able to bend a bent replaceable derailleur hanger back to its correct shape. However, because most hangers are made of aluminum, there's always a chance that trying to bend them back could result in a broken hanger.

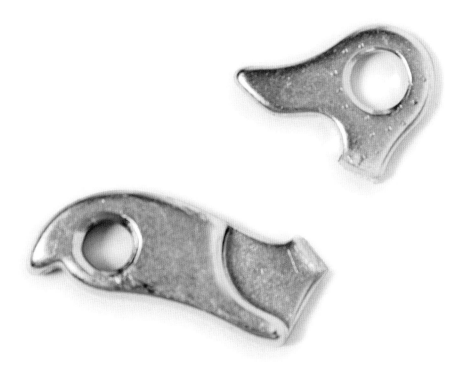

Accessory Mounts and Braze-Ons

Bicycle infrastructure is booming all over the world, and more and more riders are turning to their bikes for their main mode of transportation. Having a versatile bike makes using it easier and more enjoyable.

seatstay braze-ons enable you to mount racks and fenders to your bike

Versatility, in part, means being able to mount racks and other items onto your bike, carry things in baskets and bags attached to your bike, and ride in less-than-perfect weather with protective equipment like fenders. A bike that's constructed to do these and other tasks needs ample accessory mounts, or *braze-ons.*

One of the best additions to any bike is a rack. This simple piece of equipment enables you to ride your bike to the store for a few groceries or pedal to work without having to carry everything on your back. You can mount racks to the rear of your bike and also sometimes to the front.

Fenders are a great addition to your bike—and you don't have to ride in the rain to appreciate them. Fenders not only keep your bike cleaner in inclement weather, but they also keep you drier as they block the spray from your tires that would otherwise get your back wet. Even bikes that don't have rack mounts usually have braze-ons for fenders.

Maybe you don't want to add these accessories to your bike. Maybe all you want to add is a water bottle or a pump. Almost every bike has braze-ons for these purposes. The distance between water bottle braze-ons is a universal distance on all bikes so the two should match up, despite different brands.

Using braze-ons is really quite simple. Remove the bolt, install your accessory, add a small amount of waterproof grease to the threads of the bolt, and reinstall the bolt.

If your frame came with braze-ons but no bolts, it's not a problem. Most accessories come with all the necessary hardware. Some frames might have excess paint in the threads, which you'll need to break through before you can install the bolts. Your local bike shop should have the tool to take care of this. It's important to not try to force the bolt into the braze-on.

fork braze-ons enable you to affix racks and fenders to your bike

almost all bikes comes equipped with water bottle cage braze-ons

Almost every braze-on uses an M5x.8 bolt. If you lose a bolt and don't have extras, you can easily replace it with a high-quality stainless steel bolt from almost any hardware store.

Seat Tube Maintenance

If you never do any maintenance to your bike I would still urge you to do one thing: pull out your seatpost from time to time and add a little grease to it. In fact, seat tube maintenance is an ideal task to add to your annual service list.

Why? Because the most tedious, most time-consuming repair I can think of is trying to free a seatpost stuck in a frame. If it's not greased, once it's in there, it wants to stay in there, and getting it out can be very difficult.

Before you start this maintenance task, either measure the height of your saddle or, better yet, mark the seatpost. A felt marker or a piece of tape at the seatpost collar enables you to reinsert the post at the correct height.

1 Apply a little grease to your finger or an old toothbrush, and give your seatpost a light coating. I recommend using a lightweight, waterproof grease like Park Polylube.

2 Apply some grease inside your seat tube, too.

This is one time when I'd say there's (almost) no such thing as too much grease. Apply a good amount, and reinsert your seatpost into the frame. You can now ride with the confidence that if you ever need to remove your seatpost, it won't be a problem.

If you have a titanium frame or seatpost, antiseize lubricant might be the best choice in lubricant. Check with your bike's manufacturer for recommendations. Likewise, some carbon frame manufacturers don't recommend using grease. Specific compounds can be used in these situations instead. Again, see what your bike's maker recommends.

Cleaning Your Frame

Cleaning your bike need not be an ordeal. If it's truly dirty, you can get a bucket of warm water, some mild dish-washing soap, and a sponge and quickly clean it up. If your bike isn't in need of a full-blown bath, a rag and some cleaner works very well. You can use the same steps for either method.

You also might want to use a soft brush on the metal bits. Such brushes are available in kits, but really, an old toothbrush works just as well.

It takes a little time to do all this cleaning, but a clean bike is a happy bike!

If you use a hose to clean your bike, do *not* directly spray the bearing areas. Water will find its way beyond those seals and wash away the grease. If you have a lighter, shower setting on your hose nozzle, use that instead. And please do not take your bike to the car wash. Those high-pressure sprayers are terrible for your bike's bearings.

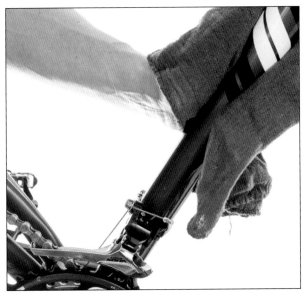

1 Start by wiping down your frame. It's the biggest area, but it's also the easiest to get clean.

2 The headtube and headset collect dirt and grime in several places, so be sure to clean both.

3 Don't forget to get the bottom bracket and the underside of the frame, too.

4 Move to your wheels next. Disconnect your brakes and remove your wheels from your bike.

5 Wipe off your front and rear brakes well. Anything your tires pick up can end up getting stuck on them, so spend a little extra time cleaning here.

Wheels seem to collect a lot of dust and dirt. Giving them a thorough cleaning not only makes them last longer but also might uncover potential service problems like broken spokes and cracked rims.

6 Next, clean all your spokes.

7 Also wipe off the rim between all the spokes. Give the hubs a wipe, too.

8 Switch to a clean rag and some solvent.

9 Using the clean rag and solvent—not cleaner or polish—clean the braking surface of the rims.

10 Using the same rag, clean in between the cogs of your cassette or freewheel.

11 If this area is really dirty, use a brush.

Inspecting Your Frame for Cracks

Nothing lasts forever, unfortunately, and sometimes bad things like cracks happen to your bike's frame.

Bike frames do develop cracks occasionally, usually in areas where two tubes are connected by a weld. Often these are found during annual tune-ups. Taking your bike to a bike shop mechanic once a year for a check-up ensures the mechanical parts are all working as they should be, and it also gives someone else the opportunity to look over your bike to spot problems you might not have seen. Chances are, a bike mechanic can detect cracks in your bike's frame you've never noticed.

This is another reason to clean your bike on a regular basis. The reason most cracks are never noticed is because they're covered in dirt. Spending some time wiping off your frame and components could potentially uncover issues before they become big problems.

Cracks appear and grow over time. That failure that happened "all of a sudden" really didn't. Luckily, most cracks never get to the point of becoming a break. If you're the bike's original owner, and it hasn't been crashed, the manufacturer will more than likely handle the issue. Take the time to look over your bike every once in a while, or have someone look it over for you—particularly right before a race or big scheduled ride.

Your frame isn't the only place on your bike that can develop cracks. Your wheels are under a great deal of stress, especially at the spoke hole on the rim. Every time you clean your bike, wipe off your rims and inspect them.

Also periodically check the threaded hole where your pedals connect to the crank, stem bolts, and seatpost clamps.

> While cracks in metal frames are serious and need to be addressed, cracks in carbon fiber frames are extremely serious. If you find a crack in your carbon bike, take it to your dealer immediately for inspection.

bottom bracket welds

welds at seat tube junction

weld below seatpost collar

spoke nipple

Dealing with Dents and Dings

Bikes are meant to be ridden, but it's a sad truth that if you ride your bike, it's eventually going to get banged up. The first one always seems to hurt the worst, but you got the bike to ride, right? Think of these dents and dings as your bike having a bit more character.

Dings, Scratches, and Chips

There are some dings you should worry about, and some you shouldn't.

If you have a metal frame, scratches and chips in the paint aren't the end of the world. No one wants a scratched bike, but scratched paint doesn't equate to structural damage or a safety issue.

You can use touch-up paint to cover a scratch. The chance of finding an exact match for the color is low, so just try to find the closest match. Covering up the scratch to protect the frame is your real goal, not necessarily making it look brand new again.

Over the years, getting touch-up paint from bike manufacturers has been a challenge. If you can't find touch-up paint, model paint from a hobby store or even nail polish make suitable replacements.

If you have a carbon frame, you need to take dings a little more seriously. First, you want to be sure the scratch doesn't get down to the frame material itself. Surface scratches can be touched up with clear nail polish. But if your carbon frame is gouged, you should take it to your bike shop for inspection.

Dents

With a dent, the seriousness partially depends on where it's located. On a metal frame, a small dent in the top tube probably isn't something to worry about. A larger dent, especially somewhere like the underside of the downtube, probably means the frame is finished. You could ride it problem free for a while, but any further impact could result in total frame failure.

When dealing with dents in carbon fiber, you have to be more careful. Because carbon fiber doesn't really dent, the damage may present itself as a chip. Treat any impact with care because there could be more damage under the surface you can't see.

Test the area by tapping around the impact with a coin. The sound should be solid all the way around. If you detect a spot where the sound is a dull thud, there's probably some underlying damage. Take your bike to your bike dealer for inspection. Unlike metal frames, carbon can fail quite unexpectedly.

Chapter 12
Suspension

Once reserved for professional or competition bikes, today, more and more personal and recreational bikes are being equipped with some sort of suspension systems that provide additional comfort for the rider. In this chapter, you learn some basic maintenance procedures for your suspension, including how to clean and lubricate it, how to ensure the setup is correct, and how to adjust sag.

Cleaning and Lubricating the Suspension

Suspension forks are available in nearly every price point. The type of suspension varies greatly, but regardless of the type of suspension your bike has, it still needs a little attention now and then.

For a suspension fork to work properly, the upper tubes need to slide freely in the lower legs. For most forks, basic maintenance is very simple and takes very little time.

1 The upper tubes of your fork will pick up quite a bit of dirt, especially if you're riding off road. Therefore, it's a very good idea to wipe off these tubes on a regular basis.

2 Some forks use oil to lubricate the lower legs and, in some cases, control part of the suspension, too. While you're wiping down the fork, check the lower legs to ensure no oil is leaking. If you find that your fork has a leak, consult your owner's manual or visit your local shop to diagnose any potential problems.

3 When you're done wiping down the fork, apply some lubricant to the upper legs. A Teflon-based chain lube works well here. Apply the lube around the dust seal between the upper tube and the lower leg.

After you apply the lube, cycle the fork up and down a few times and then wipe off any excess lube.

Suspension technology has taken quantum leaps in the last decade. Forks and shocks have gotten lighter while adding more travel (the distance your suspension moves up and down) and features. As a result, in many cases, the systems have gotten more technically complex. Many forks, for example, require specific tools for disassembly. These same forks might require multiple, specific lubricants. Always refer to your owner's manual, or consult your local bike shop, before attempting any service that requires disassembly.

Adjusting Sag

To get the most out of your suspension, it needs to be adjusted for your weight. This is true for front and rear suspensions alike. The amount your suspension compresses under your weight is called *sag*.

The amount of sag suggested varies by product and manufacturer, but a good place to start is 20 to 25 percent of the total amount of the distance your suspension moves up and down, called travel.

Note if your fork doesn't have a preload adjustment, you won't be able to adjust the sag.

1 You're going to need a way to measure the amount of travel in your fork. The easiest way to do this is to put a plastic tie around the upper tube of your fork. It should be snug but not tight.

2 Push the tie down so it is right up against the suspension's dust seal.

3 Have a friend hold your bike, and mount the bike, trying not to push down on the fork. If the zip tie moved up while you were getting on the bike, push it back down. (You want it to be down against the fork seal before you sit so you can get an accurate sag measure.) Now sit on the bike in your natural riding position.

4 Carefully get off the bike and measure the distance between the fork seal and plastic tie. This is your current amount of sag. In this example, we're using a fork with 100 millimeters travel. For this bike and this rider, this is an acceptable amount of sag. If you have a 100mm-travel fork, this would be in the right range; if you had an 80mm- or 120mm-travel fork, it would not be. The measurement varies depending on the fork.

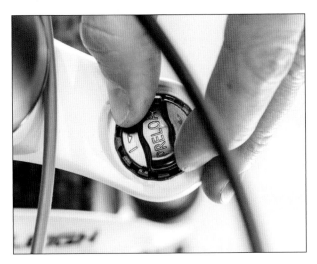

5 To adjust the amount of sag, use the preload adjustment on your fork. To reduce the amount of sag, add preload. To increase it, decrease the preload.

Chapter 13

Cranks and Bottom Brackets

The crank and bottom bracket are the heart of your bike's drivetrain. And because forward motion is initiated with these parts, you want to be sure they're in optimal working order. In this chapter, you meet the different types of bottom brackets commonly used on today's bikes. You also learn how to remove and install bottom brackets, replace crank arms, and identify worn chainrings that can greatly reduce your bike's efficiency.

Crank Arm Fixing Bolts

Crank arm fixing bolts do just that–keep your crank arms fixed, or attached, to your bicycle. That's a pretty important job. Unfortunately, these bolts are often overlooked and even neglected.

The majority of bikes still use some form of center bolt to affix the crank arms to the bottom bracket. These bolts press the arms onto the spindle. The high torque values for these bolts ensure the bolts, and crank arms, stay in place.

On a square-tapered bottom bracket, the crank arm fixing bolt wedges the crank arm onto the spindle of the bottom bracket. A loose bolt allows a crank arm to move slightly with each pedal stroke. The looser the bolt gets, the more the arm moves. Because the bottom bracket spindle is steel and the crank arm is aluminum, it doesn't take long for the hole in the arm to become deformed. This will likely cause the arm to fall off. After that, it won't ever stay on, and your only option is to replace the crank arm. But all that's avoidable if you give your crank arm fixing bolts a little attention from time to time.

An Allen wrench is all you need to check the tightness of your crank arm fixing bolts. Considering the job they do, these bolts need to be secure in order to keep your crank arms in place, so from time to time, check their tightness.

You should remove them and grease them from time to time as well.

The bigger bolt on a splined bottom bracket makes it less likely for the bolt to loosen, but it does happen. The jeopardy is the same.

Two-piece cranks use a large fixing bolt on the nondrive side. This bolt is installed by hand, and you should check it periodically to ensure it hasn't become loose.

The crank arm fixing bolts work in conjunction with the two pinch bolts on the crank arm. The torque setting on the pinch bolts is much lower, but it's still very important that they stay tight. So when you're checking your crank arm fixing bolts, use an Allen wrench to check the pinch bolts, too.

Removing Crank Arms

Knowing how to install and remove your bike's crank arms is one of the most useful skills you can have when it comes to bike repair and maintenance. Removing them enables you to access your bottom bracket, which is helpful when you want to give your drivetrain a deep clean.

The job varies slightly depending on the crank you're using and particularly how the arm attaches to your bike and the tool required to remove the arm. For example, the process of removing crank arms used with square taper bottom brackets or splined-type bottom brackets (such as Shimano Octalink or ISIS) is the same. The crank arm removal tool you need, however, is slightly different. The spindle of a splined bottom bracket is larger, so the part of the tool that pushes against the bottom bracket spindle needs to be larger as well.

Look at your bike's crank arms and the tool needed to remove them, and determine which method presented here is best for your bike.

Method One

1 Start by removing the crank arm fixing bolts using an Allen wrench.

2 Starting it by hand, thread the crank arm removal tool into the crank arm.

3 When you get it started, use a wrench to ensure the tool is fully engaged with the threads.

Failure to engage all the threads can result in you inadvertently pulling the threads out of your crank arm. So be sure you have it started correctly by hand before you get the wrench involved.

4 Rotate the crank arm removal tool clockwise to pull the crank arm off the spindle.

Because the crank arm is literally wedged onto a square taper bottom bracket, I recommend removing these arms as infrequently as possible.

Method Two

The Shimano Hollowtech crankset uses a large fixing bolt and pinch bolts to secure the nondrive-side-only crank arm.

1 Start by loosening the pinch bolts on the crank arm using an Allen wrench.

2 Next, using a flathead screwdriver, dislodge the safety tab on the crank arm.

Other cranks use the same method of attachment, but Shimano is the only brand that uses a safety tab. The tab interacts with a hole in the spindle and must be removed before you can take off the crank arm.

3 Next, remove the crank arm fixing bolt. It should be only be in hand-tight, so you shouldn't need any wrenches here.

4 After you've loosened the bolts, the crank arm should slide off the spindle.

5 To remove the drive-side crank arm, remove the chain and pull the arm through the bottom bracket.

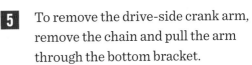

A Look at Bottom Brackets

In the same way that your hubs allow your wheels to rotate, your bike's bottom bracket allows your pedals to rotate. The bottom bracket is a combination of bearings and a spindle that are inserted through the bottom bracket shell of your bike's frame. Given the amount of torque that's applied to the pedals, you and your bike both demand a lot from this small component.

Cup and Cone Bottom Brackets

Early bottom brackets operated with a cup and cone, much like a hub. These bottom brackets are still found on some entry-level or department store bikes, but they have largely fallen out of favor.

In an attempt to constantly make bikes lighter, manufacturers continually modify bottom bracket designs.

Square Taper Bottom Brackets

The square tapered, cartridge-bearing bottom bracket could be the most used bottom bracket in the bicycle world. This design was an improvement over the cup and cone bottom bracket because the bearings and spindle were combined into one sealed unit. This makes installation and adjustment easier, and it makes them much more weather resistant. In most cases, the drive-side cup is attached to the unit, leaving the nondrive side (or adjustable) cup loose. Even the relatively inexpensive models provide years of trouble-free service.

There's only one potential downside to this type of bottom bracket: repeated installation and removal of an aluminum crank arm on a steel spindle could deform the hole where the crank mounts to the spindle. This could lead to the inability to fully tighten the arm to the spindle. In extreme cases, the arm could fall off all together.

Splined Bottom Brackets

The few problems with square tapered spindles led to the development of the splined bottom bracket. The larger, splined spindle provides a more secure connection between the crank arm and the spindle. The hollow spindle also makes it possible to make the bottom bracket slightly lighter.

Beyond that, this type of bracket shares all the characteristics of the square tapered version.

External Bottom Brackets

The next step in bottom brackets came from an effort to make the bottom bracket area not only lighter, but also stiffer. The development of products like the Shimano Hollowtech crank took the bottom bracket spindle and attached it to the drive-side crank arm. This made the spindle larger and lighter, and moving the bearings outside the bottom bracket shell made the whole system stiffer.

These bearings are easy to install, relatively weather resistant, and sufficiently durable.

Press Fit Bottom Brackets

The last step in the current evolution has widened the bottom bracket shell and pushed the bearings back inside the shell. Press fit bottom brackets might be the lightest bottom brackets yet. They essentially use the same bearings found in the external cups.

Time will tell if the lack of a cup and threaded connection with the frame will affect durability.

Measuring the Bottom Bracket Spindle Width

When it comes time to replace your bottom bracket, you must take two important measurements into consideration. The first is the width of your bike's bottom bracket shell, and the second is the length of the bottom bracket spindle.

Most bikes today have a bottom bracket shell that's either 68 millimeters or 73 millimeters. This one is 73 millimeters.

You need to know the width of the shell when you're replacing your bottom bracket because the spindle length corresponds to the crankset you're using on your bike. This, in turn, affects the chain line, which affects shifting.

Most manufacturers list the appropriate spindle length for each of their cranksets, sometimes on the middle of the bottom bracket. If you see a size of 68×112, for example, that means the bracket is for a bike with a 68-millimeter shell and the spindle is 112 millimeters long. If the size isn't listed, you'll need to measure it.

These measurements become doubly important if you're replacing components on your bike. Your crank, bottom bracket, and front derailleur all need to work together. If you're changing from one crankset to another, you might have to replace more than just the crank. Be sure to check the manufacturer's specifications for required chain line on all the parts you're replacing.

Note this information does not apply to a bike that has an external cup or press fit bottom bracket.

Removing and Installing Bottom Brackets

Having the capability to remove and replace your bottom bracket is helpful for a number of reasons. Even the best bottom brackets eventually wear out. And if you ride in muddy conditions or get caught in a torrential rain, it's great to be able to pull off the bottom bracket, clean it, and apply some new grease when you get home.

A good cleaning and new grease also can solve some of the popping and creaking you might be hearing from your bike. (It doesn't all come from the bottom bracket, but it tends to get most of the blame.)

External Cup Bottom Brackets

If you have a bottom bracket with external cups, this is a pretty straightforward operation.

You'll need the tool for your specific bottom bracket and a torque wrench.

With all threaded bottom brackets, the drive side of the bike has a reverse thread. Using your bottom bracket tool and a socket wrench, remove the cup from the frame.

If your bike has an Italian bottom bracket, it will have right-hand thread on both sides.

When reinstalling an external cup bottom bracket, it's important that you start screwing on the cups by hand. Remember, the drive side has a reverse thread.

Once the cups are hand-tight, use your bottom bracket tool and torque wrench to tighten the cups to the manufacturer's torque specifications.

Square Taper and Splined Bottom Brackets

If you have a square taper or splined cartridge bottom bracket, the steps are very similar but the tool is different.

Remove the adjustable cup first. Remember, the drive-side cup is usually the fixed cup (attached to the bottom bracket), but not in all cases. Then remove the fixed cup along with the bottom bracket.

When it's time to reinstall the bottom bracket, start both cups by hand. Turn the adjustable cup in one or two threads only. Using your bottom bracket tool and a torque wrench, tighten the fixed cup down to the manufacturer's torque specifications. To finish the job, tighten the adjustable cup to the recommended torque specifications.

Some adjustable cups have a lip on them and some don't. Your torque wrench tells you when you're done tightening. Usually you reach the manufacturer's recommended torque settings before the cups reach the frame.

Chainring Fixing Bolts

Checking your chainring fixing bolts is a good thing to add to your regular maintenance routine. Any fixing bolt can loosen over time, and chainring bolts are no different.

If you have a triple chainring, the smallest ring attaches directly to the crank arm with a chainring bolt. You can adjust the bolt using an Allen wrench.

There may be times when you can remove your chainring bolts without the nut tool. It's less likely, however, that you can fully tighten the bolts without one.

To tighten, loosen, or remove the bolts on the other chainrings, you need an Allen wrench and a chainring nut tool. This pronged tool enables you to hold the nut so you can adjust the bolt.

Once you can adjust these bolts, you also can replace your chainrings. This is an advantage if, for example, you had a compact crank and wanted to replace the small 34-tooth ring with a 39-tooth ring. Changing cassettes is usually the method used to customize gearing, and replacing a chainring may provide the desired result—at a lower cost.

Use a small amount of grease when reinstalling the chainring bolts. And tighten bolts gradually to ensure each bolt is tightened evenly.

Whenever possible, try to make these adjustments without taking the crank off the bike.

Cranksets

These days, you have a lot more choices when it comes to gearing. When I first started riding a road bike, I rode a standard double. It wasn't even called "standard" back then; it was just a double. You had two chainrings on the front of your bike, and they were 52/42. After some time, that morphed into 53/39. (52/42 refers to the number of teeth on your largest and smallest chainrings. In this example, the largest chainring has 52 teeth and the smallest chainring has 42 teeth.)

As cycling became more mainstream, recreational cyclists began to find that the gearing racers used wasn't compatible with their sometimes-slower pace and more leisurely rides—the gearing choices were too narrow, and the bikes were generally geared too tall (hard).

In response, triples started showing up on what were historically thought of as racing bikes. These were the early days of dual-control levers, and with a triple, they just didn't shift all that well. Racers continued to turn up their noses, and the recreational riders became frustrated. Enter the "compact" crank.

The Compact Crankset

The compact crankset uses a 50-tooth large chainring and a 34-tooth small ring (50/34). It was designed to provide roughly the same range of gearing as a triple with the shifting performance of a double. It sounded great from the start, and in large part, it still is.

If you have a bike with a standard double, you might be thinking, *This sounds great! I'll just switch my chainrings for the smaller, compact sizes.* Not so fast. This is where B.C.D. comes in. *B.C.D.* stands for "Bolt Circle Diameter" and is the diameter of the circle formed by your chainring bolts. The standard crank has a B.C.D. of 130 millimeters. The compact has a B.C.D. of 110 millimeters. To make that switch, you'd have to replace the entire crankset, not just the rings.

The compact crank is not without its own issues. If you live in an area that's relatively flat, the 34-tooth small chainring is so small, it's nearly unusable. You're likely to spend all your time in the big chainring—effectively halving the number of gears on your bike.

Moreover, using the small ring means that most front shifts really become double shifts. A rear gear that's hard enough in the small chainring is *too* hard when you switch to the big ring. If you live in an area with a lot of long, gradual climbs, the gearing of the compact cranks might work very well for you.

compact crankset

triple crankset

The Updated Triple Crankset

A year or so after the compact crank became available, an exciting thing happened: the gearing on triples changed. Road bikes with triple chainrings are now 50/39/30, with a very usable middle chainring with a "bail-out" gear.

These cranks use a B.C.D. of 110 millimeters, just like the compacts, with a B.C.D. of 74 millimeters for the smallest chainring.

This is the ideal setup for the recreational cyclist. You can run a relatively narrow spacing of gears in the back, which minimizes big jumps between the gears. You have a big ring that is, for most riders, plenty big enough, and you have a gear in which to climb hills. Add to that the improved shifting performance of current dual-control levers, and you've got a winning combination.

The bottom line is that there's no perfect gearing, but the choices and combinations have never been greater. It might take some time to figure out what the best set up is for you, but it's worth your time to figure it out.

Recognizing Wear

When your chain, chainrings, and cogs are new, they mesh together with each roller of the chain putting equal pressure on its corresponding tooth.

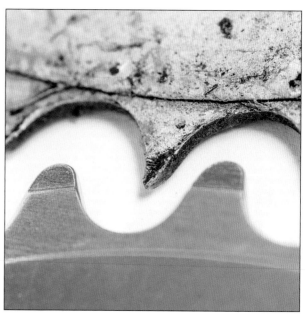

Over time, however, and as the chain stretches, the teeth on the chainrings and cogs wear along with it. A badly stretched chain will eventually wear to such an extent that the rollers of the chain no longer mesh with the teeth of the chainrings and cogs. The result is chain slippage and poor shifting. If left unchecked for too long, you might have to replace both your chain and your chainrings or cogs if they become irrevocably damaged.

Given their size, the chainrings on the front of your bike contact the chain less frequently than smaller cassette cogs at the back of your bike. This results in slower wear, but it can still be minimized with proper chain maintenance.

The most important thing you can do is check the wear of your chain regularly. "Regularly" depends on how much you ride. If you ride every day, check your chain a couple times a year. If you're more of a casual rider, once a year is sufficient.

Checking your chain for wear is a job you can quickly do with a chain checker. Your local bike shop should have one, or you can purchase this tool if you prefer to check your chain more often. Compatible with all bike chains, a chain checker attaches to two links in your chain and measures wear and stretch.

Most new bikes have chainrings that are ramped and beveled. Although these are sometimes mistaken for broken teeth, they're meant to be this way. The profiled chainring teeth assist in front shifting.

Chapter 14

Accessorizing Your Bike

Accessories are a great way to personalize your bike, and they can add a great deal of functionality as well. In this chapter, you learn how to properly install many useful items, including water bottle cages, pumps, racks, fenders, lights, baskets, bags, and cycling computers, that can turn your bike into more than just two wheels that get you from point A to point B.

Adding Water Bottle Cages

One of the most useful things you can add to your bike is also one of the easiest. When you're out riding, you might get hot, and you're certainly going to get thirsty. Enter the water bottle cage.

1 Using an Allen wrench—try a 4-millimeter or 5-millimeter size—to loosen the bolts.

2 It's always a good idea to put a little grease on the threads while you have the bolts out.

Nearly every bike has one or sometimes even two sets of water bottle braze-ons that hold a standard bicycle water bottle cage. The distance between the braze-ons is one of the few consistent things on all bikes, regardless of the brand.

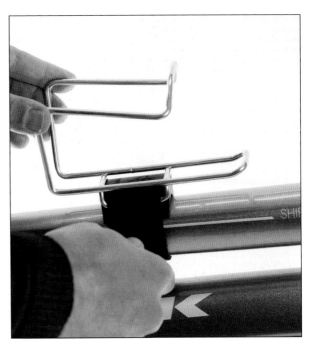

3 Line up the holes in the water bottle cage with the holes in your frame, and reinstall the bolts.

Some frames don't have these threaded braze-ons. You can still have a drink while riding by using a water bottle cage that mounts to the frame with Velcro.

Installing Frame Pumps

Part of everyone's road repair kit should include some way to inflate a new tube after you get a flat tire. Because of its small size and convenient mounting options, the mini pump is very popular. It provides all the needed inflation you need for emergency situations, and when you don't need it, it stows out of the way.

If you have an unused set of water bottle braze-ons, you can use them to mount a mini pump.

You need an Allen wrench to unscrew the bolts. Apply a thin layer of grease to the bolts while you have them out.

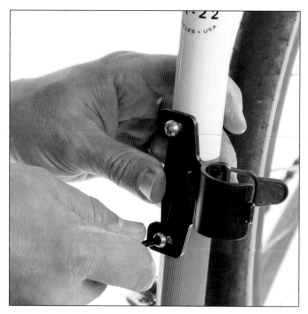

1 Line up the holes in the pump bracket with the holes in your frame, and reinstall the bolts.

2 Insert the pump into the bracket, and you're ready to go.

If both sets of bosses are being used, you can mount the bracket under one of your water bottle cages.

Mounting mini pumps to your frame isn't your only option. Some are so small they fit in a larger seat bag. If you ride a mountain bike, or if you want your pump to be protected from the elements, this might be a consideration for you.

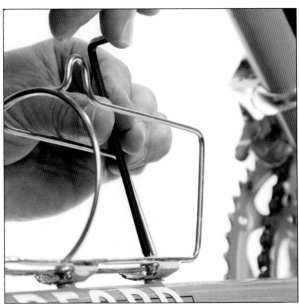

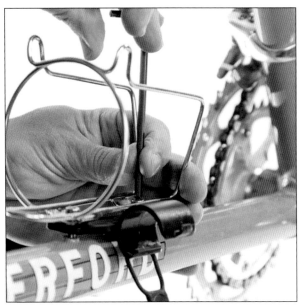

1 Unscrew the bolts holding your water bottle cage to your frame.

2 Layer the pump bracket under the water bottle cage, line up the holes in both with the holes in your frame, and reinstall the bolts. (Most pumps come with longer bolts for this use should you need them.)

Adding Racks

I admit it—I love racks on a bike. When I see them, I know the person who owns the bike values it as a legitimate form of transportation. Front and rear racks equip your bike to carry more than just you. They might seem complicated, but today's better bike racks are actually quite easy to install.

Attaching a Rear Rack

Installing rear racks is pretty straightforward.

1 Position the rack over the back tire.

2 Attach the rack to the eyelets on the rear dropout. Do not fully tighten the bolts.

3 Attach the struts to the upper eyelets, ensuring the upper struts don't interfere with your brakes, but leave the bolts that attach the struts to the rack loose.

4 Move the rack until it's level, and tighten all the bolts to secure the rack in place.

You might need to shorten the struts on some racks. If you have one of these racks, you'll have some additional installation steps. When the rack is leveled, mark the struts, remove them from the rack, shorten them according to the manufacturer's instructions, and reinstall them.

Attaching a Front Rack

Rear racks may be more common, but you can take your bike to the next level of usefulness by adding a front rack. Front racks are great for supporting a bag or providing another place on your bike to strap something bulky but light. You can mount a rack to the front of your bike in a couple different ways.

Some front racks look very similar to a rear rack but are shorter. If the fork dropouts have eyelets, these racks work well.

1 Start by attaching the struts to these eyelets, leaving the bolts loose enough so you can level the rack later.

2 Attach the rack to the underside of the fork crown. Depending on the way your rack mounts, you might have to modify the brace slightly to work around the headset's lower cup.

3 Attach the brace to the center hole in your fork crown. Use the supplied hardware to make this attachment, or as we've shown here, use the hardware in conjunction with your fender hardware.

4 Be sure your rack is level before tightening all the bolts.

If you don't have lower fork eyelets, but you have cantilever (or linear pull) brakes, some front racks will work with your bike. Using these racks requires mounting the rack directly to the brake braze-ons.

1 Start by removing the bolts from your brakes.

2 Apply some grease on the brake braze-ons, put your rack in place, and reinstall the bolts.

3 Install the brace to the center of the rack (if it wasn't preinstalled), leaving the bolts loose. Level your rack and tighten everything in place.

4 Once the rack is in place, attach the rack brace to the fork crown.

Fastening on Fenders

You would never drive your car without fenders. Yet it's common for bikes to go without. Fenders keep you dry when the roads are wet, and they provide a valuable service even when conditions are dry by keeping your bike cleaner.

Installing a Rear Fender

Mounting a fender on your back tire takes a few steps but is still pretty easy.

1 Start by removing your rear wheel.

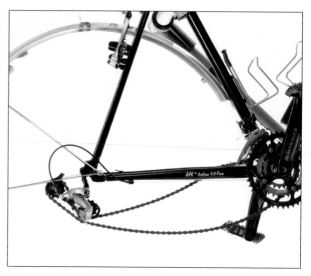

2 Insert the fender in its approximate location, and line it up with the braze-ons.

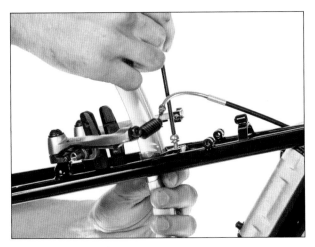

3 Attach the fender at the seatstay bridge. This supports the fender so you can make adjustments to the spacing.

4 With the fender supported, attach the fender to the chainstay bridge.

5 Now attach the fender braces to the rear dropout eyelets.

6 Reinstall your wheel, and reconnect the brake. You should have a consistent gap between the fender and the tire. When you're satisfied with the adjustment, tighten all the bolts.

Attaching a Front Fender

Attaching a fender to your front tire is easier than attaching one on the rear tire.

1 You might have to bend the mounting tab to clear the bottom cup of your headset. Using a pair of pliers, gently bend the tab as necessary to fit your bike.

2 Using the supplied hardware, insert the bolt through the mounting bracket, ...

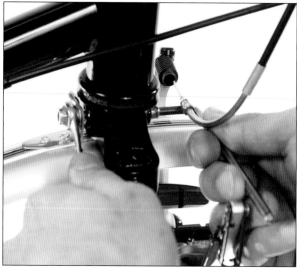

3 ... and tighten the bolt.

4 Attach the fender struts to the lower eyelets of your fork.

5 With all the hardware attached, reinsert your wheel to check the fender clearance and reconnect the brakes. Adjust the fender if necessary, and fully tighten all hardware.

Now the next rainy day doesn't have to keep you off your bike.

To achieve the desired fender line, you might need to use a spacer between the fender and the chainstay bridge. A slice or chunk of cork, such as one from a wine bottle, is especially useful in this instance. Also, be sure your fenders don't interfere with your brakes. Before hitting the road on a bike with a newly installed fender, give the wheels a spin and double-check that your braking isn't hindered in any way.

Installing Lights

Putting lights on your bike has never been easier, and the lights on the market today are far brighter than lights of the past. Battery and bulb technology also has improved, providing incredibly powerful lights in amazingly small packages—perfect for installing on your bike.

If you ride at night, it's safer to ride with lights. Given the efficiency of modern LED lights, you can even ride with them on during daylight hours. Anything that makes you more noticeable as a cyclist is beneficial.

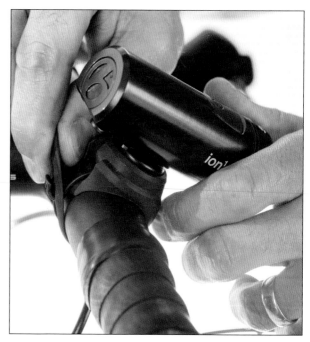

Most lights come with a bracket that easily clips on your handlebars.

Just place the light where you want it, and wrap the supplied rubber strap around your handlebars to secure the light.

If your handlebar is already crowded, or you just want to get the light closer to the ground, try mounting the light to the leg of your fork. As long as it's pointed forward, lighting your way and making you noticeable to others on the road, that's what matters.

Because most car and truck drivers see you first from the rear when you're riding on the road with them, a rear light becomes equally, if not more, important than a headlight.

Most rear lights come with brackets and rubber shims for quick and easy seatpost mounting.

You're not limited to mounting a rear light on your seatpost. You can clip lights to some seat bags, too. Or you can modify the brackets for seatstay mounting.

Attaching Baskets

The bicycle basket is the most underappreciated, underused accessory there is. A basket immediately makes your bike more usable and is a natural addition on any recreational bike.

Many different types of baskets are available, and you can mount them in many ways. Here you learn how to install a traditional basket in the traditional way.

1 Start by mounting the basket bracket to your handlebars.

2 Center the brackets, install the hardware, and snug the bolts.

3 Attach the lower struts, which support whatever weight is in the basket, to the bottom of the basket.

4 The basket needs to be supported by the front axle. On this bike, we remove the axle bolts, install the struts, and reinstall the nuts by hand.

5 Fully tighten the axle nuts, and check to be sure the basket is level.

6 When you're happy with the placement of your basket, tighten the rest of the hardware to secure the basket.

Don't use this method of attachment for quick-release axles. Lower rack eyelets can be used instead if they're available.

Mounting Computers

Especially when you first start riding, it's great to be able to see how fast you're riding or how far you've ridden. A cycling computer gives you this information and more in a small, easy-to-install package.

To mount most computers, all you need is a small screwdriver and a pair of cutters.

1 Start by installing the mounting harness to your handlebar. Use the included rubber shims to ensure a snug fit.

2 With a wired computer, the biggest challenge is dealing with the excess wire while leaving enough slack in it to turn the handlebars. The brake cable provides a nice place to secure the top of the wire. Most computers come with plastic ties for this purpose.

Most computer harnesses have the option to mount the computer on your stem. This is handy if your handlebar is already crowded. Check to be sure the stem is long enough to hold the harness, and remove the computer from the harness before installing it in this manner.

3 To keep the wire from just dangling off the bike as you ride, wind it around the cable.

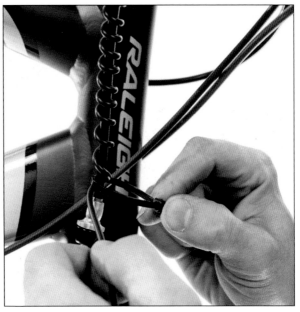

4 Using another plastic tie, secure the wire at the bottom of the cable to keep everything snug.

5 Attach the sensor to a point on the fork. It doesn't matter where on the fork you place the sensor. Just be sure the magnet is close enough to the sensor.

6 Secure the excess wire to the fork.

7 Don't forget to cut the ends off all the plastic ties.

8 Attach the magnet to your spokes, being sure to line up the magnet with the sensor.

9 Calibrate the computer based on your bike's tire size. Many computers are now preset with all common tire sizes.

10 Place the computer in the mounting harness, give the wheel a spin to be sure everything is lined up, and you're done!

Attaching Bags

Bags for your bike come in all shapes and sizes. Whether you want to carry a little or a lot, bags are available to hold what you want to hold.

Attaching a Seat Bag

The seat bag is the most common type of bag. Typically used for a spare tube and repair kit, they fit nicely under the saddle and are out of the way until you need to access them. A seat bag should be installed so it fits up against the rails of the saddle.

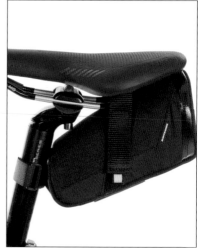

1 Loop the top Velcro strap across the rails of your saddle and cinch up tight.

2 Wrap the bottom strap around the seatpost and tighten to secure.

3 The seat bag should fit tightly up under your saddle.

Attaching a Rack-Top Bag

If you want to carry a bit more and you have a rear rack, you might want to consider a rack-top bag. The most common type of rack-top bag affixes to the rack via Velcro straps.

1 Position the bag on your rear rack, thread the straps through the rack, and cinch to secure.

2 Wrap the strap around the seatstays or seatpost and tighten.

3 Your rack-top bag is now ready to carry whatever you want to stow in it.

Attaching a Pannier

If you commute to work or use your bike to go to the store, a pannier is an ideal choice. These bags usually come in pairs and mount to the sides of your rear rack. You can mount panniers in two ways. The first uses an elastic cord to secure the bottom of the bag, and the second uses an adjustable clip to keep the bag from swaying.

1 Position one pannier on one side of your rear rack.

2 Affix the bottom pannier clip to the bottom of the rack, or secure the adjustable clip if that's what your pannier has.

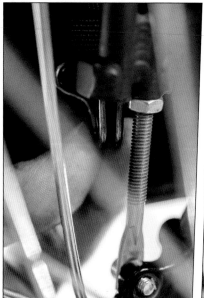 

3 Clip the top of the bag in place on the rack.

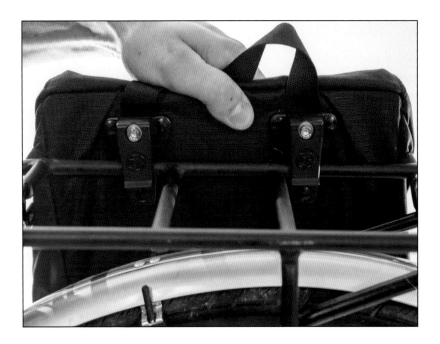

4 Repeat the procedure on the other side of your rack for the second pannier, and you're ready to hit the road.

Chapter 15

Emergency Road Repairs

Crazy things happen to your bike sometimes. It doesn't matter if you're riding on smooth roads or out on an adventurous trail. Sometimes things just happen. So what do you do? First, you don't panic. Then you assess the situation and use the handy tips in this chapter to fix the problem so you can get home.

Fixing a Cut Tire

Let's say you're out on the road and your tire gets cut so badly you can't continue to ride on it as is. What do you do?

Hopefully you carry some money with you when you ride. (If you don't, make it a point to put some paper money in your pocket or seat bag the next time you ride.) That money is good for more than just a cold drink or snack when you're out on the road or trail.

> With this fix, you should use just enough pressure to not pinch your tube. The paper money is strong, but it's not that strong.

1 Fold the paper money in half from top to bottom and then in half again from side to side. You want it to be at least four layers thick.

2 Slide the folded money between the tire and the tube, being sure to place it where the cut in the tire is.

Because paper money isn't really paper—depending on your currency, it could be a blend of cotton and linen fibers or cellulose—it should keep the tube from blowing through the tire until you can get back home.

The paper money solution to a cut tire is one of the oldest tricks around—because it works!

Fixing a Broken Spoke

A broken spoke is a frequent occurrence. Sometimes they break in such a way there's a danger of the broken spoke getting caught up in the wheel. In these situations, you have two choices.

If you can get at the spoke nipple, you might be able to loosen the spoke and remove it from the wheel.

A broken spoke can throw off a wheel's tension. If your rim now hits the brake pad, open your brake caliper to give the wheel some extra room. Just remember you're not going to have the same braking power.

In some cases, you can't turn the nipple. To fix this so you can ride again, wind the broken spoke around an adjacent, unbroken spoke.

Fixing a Twisted Chain

Getting a twisted chain while you're riding your bike doesn't happen very often, but when it does, it can put an end to your day quickly. But all is not lost. There's a chance you can get back on the road if your bike has quick-release axles.

1 Remove both quick-release skewers from your wheels, if you have them. Set aside the acorn nuts and springs—do not lose the springs!

2 Try to straighten the chain by inserting the quick-release skewers into the links adjacent to the twist and moving the skewers as necessary to straighten the chain.

By doing this, there's a good probability you can get the chain straight enough to use in some of your gears—there's no way to tell for sure which so you have to experiment. If you do, take the direct route back home, and don't put too much pressure on the chain.

Fixing a Bent Derailleur Hanger

If you twisted your chain, there's a good chance you also bent your derailleur hanger. This is a trickier fix. Depending on how badly the hanger is bent, trying to bend it back could break it. But you're not going anywhere with your hanger bent, so you might as well try to correct it.

You're going to use the derailleur bolt to try to straighten the hanger.

Straighten the Allen wrench of your multitool, insert it into the derailleur mounting bolt, and tighten it if necessary. With the wrench still in the bolt, and holding it in place, use your other hand to gently but firmly attempt to pull out the hanger.

acorn nut   The nut on the end of a quick-release skewer.

adjustable cup   The (generally) left cup of your bottom bracket that allows for adjustment.

adjusting barrel   A hollow bolt that carries a cable and includes a cable stop for the housing. This allows for fine adjustment of cable tension without the use of tools.

anchor bolt   A bolt that clamps the end of a brake or derailleur cable, holding it in place.

axle   The central shaft that goes through a wheel.

B tension   Terminology coined by bike manufacturer Shimano to describe the screw used to adjust the height of the upper pulley on a rear derailleur.

B.C.D.   Short for Bolt Circle Diameter, or the diameter of the circle formed by your chainring bolts.

bead   The part of a clincher tire that interfaces with the rim. It's usually made of steel or Kevlar.

bottom bracket   The bearings, or bearings and spindle, that enable the crank arms to rotate.

cable   The steel wire that controls shifting and braking. Used in conjunction with cable housing.

cable stop   A fitting found on components and frames that stops the cable housing but allows the cable to pass though.

caliper   The brakes found on most road bikes.

cantilever brake   Brakes that feature two independently operating arms that connect to posts, or braze-ons, located on the fork or frame of the bicycle.

cassette   A cluster of cogs or sprockets that connect to the freehub body of a rear hub.

chain   The device used by most modern bikes to transmit power and drive the rear wheel.

chain line   The gauge of how straight the chain runs between the front and rear sprockets.

chainstays   The tubes of the frame that run from the bottom bracket shell to the rear dropouts.

chain whip   The tool used to keep the freehub from spinning while you remove the cassette lock ring.

chainring   The front sprockets of a bicycle.

cleat   The piece that, when fitted to a shoe, enables your shoe to connect to the pedal.

clincher tire   A tire that uses a separate inner tube. The tire features a bead that allows it to stay connected to the rim.

clipless pedals   Pedals that connect to your shoe without the need for toe clips or straps.

compact crank   A double crankset that allows for the use of smaller chainrings.

crankset   The total of both crank arms and chainrings.

derailleur   The mechanism that moves the chain from one gear to another.

dish   The term used to describe the adjustment made to wheels to ensure they're centered in the frame.

down tube   The tube of a bicycle frame that runs from the head tube to the bottom bracket shell.

drop handlebar   The type of handlebar found on most road bikes. The center of the bar is straight, and it then bends down and back toward the rider.

dropout   The part of the frame or fork where the wheel is attached.

dual-pivot brake   A type of caliper brake in which the arms of the brake are linked together.

fork   The part of the bicycle that holds the front wheel.

frame   The central part of a bicycle to which the wheels and all other components connect.

freehub   The Shimano trademark for the freewheeling body of a cassette hub.

freewheel   The mechanism that, when threaded onto a rear hub, allows for coasting on a geared bicycle.

headset   The component that connects the fork to the frame and enables the fork to turn.

headtube   The front tube of the frame.

hub   The middle part of the wheel. Bearings held inside the hub allow the wheel to spin.

limit screw   The screws that set the limit of how far the derailleur can move left or right.

linear pull brake   A type of cantilever brake that doesn't use a straddle or straddle cable.

master link   A special link used to connect and disconnect a chain. Also used to describe the connecting link used on geared bicycle chains.

nipple   The nut that connects the end of a spoke to the wheel's rim.

noodle   The curved piece of tubing that connects the cable to a linear pull brake.

over locknut dimension (O.L.D.)   The distance between the outside of the hub lock nuts.

pedal   The part of the bike where your foot rests. The pedal's spindle connects to the crank arm.

pinch flat   A flat caused by the tube getting pinched between the rim and another hard object. This is most often caused by riding on underinflated tires.

pitch   The distance between the rollers of a chain.

Presta valve   The narrow valve used on most higher-end bikes. The valve is recognizable by the exposed nut used to open and close the valve.

quick-release lever   A cam lever used to remove a bicycle wheel without tools.

race   The part of a bicycle on which a ball bearing rolls.

rim   The hoop that, along with the spokes and a hub, makes up a wheel.

saddle   The part of the bike you sit on. It's most often referred to as a seat.

sag   The amount your suspension compresses under your weight.

Schrader valve   An automotive-style valve used on entry-level to mid-priced bicycles.

seat tube   The center tube of the frame that connects to the bottom bracket shell.

seatpost   The pillar that's inserted into the frame and holds the saddle of your bike.

seatstay   The tubes of the frame that connect between the top of the seat tube to the rear dropouts.

shifter   The mechanism that initiates gear shifts.

single-pivot brake   The traditional type of caliper brake.

spoke   The wire that connects the hub to the rim. Better-quality spokes are made of stainless steel.

stem   The part of the bike that connects the handlebars to the fork's steerer tube.

threaded headset   The traditional type of headset in which the top race and lock nut thread onto the steerer of the fork.

threadless headset   The type of headset used on most current bikes. The upper race slides over a smooth fork steerer.

tire lever   Tools made of plastic or metal that pry the bead of a tire off the wheel's rim.

top tube   The tube of a frame that runs from the headtube to the seat tube.

torque wrench   A wrench used to determine how much torque is being applied to fasteners.

travel   The distance your suspension moves up and down.

wheel   An assembled rim, spokes, and hub. May also include a tire and inner tube.

MAINTENANCE SCHEDULES

Now that you're better equipped to perform maintenance tasks on your bike, you can catch small issues before they become big problems.

In this appendix, I share my suggested daily, monthly, and annual maintenance schedules.

Daily Maintenance

- [ ] Before every ride, do a walk-around of your bike to check for anything out of place or in need of repair.

- [ ] Give the wheels a spin and be sure your tires are inflated.

- [ ] After you've inflated your tires, lift the front wheel off the ground and give it a bounce. Did you hear anything other than the tire hitting the ground? If so, it could be a cable, a loose Presta valve nut, or your headset. Check it out, and tighten whatever's loose.

Monthly Maintenance

- [ ] Keep your bike clean. Dirt can cause wear faster than anything else. Few people clean their bikes after every ride, but a monthly cleaning goes a long way toward making your bike last longer. Simply wipe down your frame and clean the chain, and your bike will look a lot better and shift more smoothly.

- [ ] While you're wiping down your bike, inspect the frame and wheels for cracks. Be sure no problems are hiding under the dirt.

- [ ] Get rid of any squeaks in your chain by applying some lubrication to it. This is especially important if you've just cleaned your chain. Remember, a little goes a long way.

- [ ] Be sure your wheels are sound. Check them for cuts, and give them a spin to be sure they're true. Check for any loose or broken spokes, too.

- [ ] Vibration that happens out on the road or trail has a way of loosening bolts. Check all fasteners to be sure they're tight.

- [ ] It's important that you're able to stop when you need to. Check your brake pads for wear.

- [ ] Inspect your cables. Replace any cables that are showing signs of rust or fraying.

- [ ] Take care of your suspension by checking all pivot bolts. Be sure they're all torqued to the manufacturer's specifications.

Annual Maintenance

- ☐ If you have an off season, that's the perfect time to do some larger maintenance jobs. Then your bike will be ready to roll when you're ready to get back in the saddle.

- ☐ Overhaul any loose ball components. Apply new grease in all those bearing areas—especially important for those loose-ball hubs.

- ☐ Freshen up an older bike with new handlebar tape or grips. Clean tape or grips make your bike look like new—and it's a simple task to complete.

- ☐ Inspect all cables and housing, and replace any cables and housing that are showing wear. At a minimum, replace the small piece of shift housing at the rear derailleur.

- ☐ Check for chain stretch. If the chain is at or near 1 percent stretch, it's time for a new chain.

- ☐ Remove the crank, cassette, and chain, and give your drivetrain a thorough cleaning.

- ☐ Pull the seatpost, and add some lube. There's nothing worse than a seatpost that won't come out when you want it to.

- ☐ Replace any worn brake pads.

- ☐ Take a look inside your seat bag. Replace any tubes of CO_2 cartridges that were used and not replaced. Out on the road is not the time to find out you're missing a critical piece of your emergency kit.

- ☐ If you use a cycling computer or any other accessory that requires batteries, replace them. This probably isn't something you need to do every year, but batteries are less expensive than having your electronics quit in the middle of a big ride or race.

INDEX

A

Photography by Greg Perez, with the following exceptions:

4, 5   (red, white, and blue racing bike) Philip Gatward © Dorling Kindersley

7   (vise) Gerard Brown © Dorling Kindersley

7   (toolbox) Dave King © Dorling Kindersley

56, 57   (illustrations) Kevin James Associates © Dorling Kindersley

92   (chains) Gerard Brown © Dorling Kindersley

103   (red, white, and blue racing bike) Philip Gatward © Dorling Kindersley